# LIGHT THE FIRE!

*Inspire &
Impact Kids!*

## LANE WALKER

*Light the Fire: Inspire and Impact Kids*
by Lane Walker
Copyright © 2021 Lane Walker

ISBN: 978-1-955657-13-6
For Worldwide Distribution
Printed in the U.S.A.

Published by Bakken Books
2021
www.lanewalkerbooks.com

# DEDICATION

I BELIEVE THAT EVERY child is a gift from God and should be cherished and nurtured. Every kid, regardless of circumstances and life events, is special. There are no exceptions or deviations in my belief. Kids need adults in their life to invest and believe in them. Some simply need one caring adult to change their world in a positive way. You could be that one person!

Thankfully, I have had multiple people invest in me. This book is a culmination of those people and students who daily help me see the potential in every kid. These strategies and principles have helped me make connections with even the toughest of students. My inspiration for writing this book is simple: I want the book to help bridge a relationship and make a positive impact in a kid's life.

I have had countless people believe in and support me. My parents have and always will be the driving force behind my success. They taught me morals and values that sustained me even through difficult times. The lessons and example they provide prepared me for life. I will always be thankful for my mom's making Sunday morning church a priority and for my dad's knocking on my door at 3:30 a.m. for hunting adventures. They always fanned the flames and made sure my fire was burning bright. They always let me be me! Thanks to my brother for sharing the cereal and teaching me how to throw pinecones and all the other life lessons.

My wife and children have been the greatest gift I have ever received. My three daughters, Gracy, Abby and Molly, bring me unmatched joy and show me grace and humility on a daily basis. My girls own a piece of real estate in my heart that will never be for sale or lose value. My son, Rece, brings me endless happiness. I wake up every day and am so thankful for him. I love fishing, throwing the football and watching cartoons with him. Having a little boy has taught me so much, and I continue to grow and learn more every day. My wife is one of the best teachers I have ever seen. Her endless late nights worrying about her students, never-give-up attitude and passion drive me. She is a constant encourager and has a direct, positive impact on kids every day. We both share a strong belief that every kid matters and is capable of great things. She sets out to prove that and to inspire students every day.

I am a small-town homemade person. Growing up, I had so many adults, teachers and coaches invest in me and light my fire for life. The people who live in my hometown of Kingston have had a huge impact on my life journey. I am proud of where I was raised and proud to still be a part of it.

To all the adults, relatives and coaches who believed in me, thank you. Your love and support have helped me in more ways than I can began to describe.

## DEDICATION

Lastly, this book is dedicated to all the educators and students with whom I have had the privilege of working the past 20 years. Those students have provided me with so many intrinsic rewards.

Thank you for helping me realize that sometimes all a kid needs is one loving adult to light his or her fire.

# Table of Contents

# FOREWORD

by Mark C. Perna

*International Speaker, Author, and CEO*

*Bestselling Winner of 8 National Awards*

The world has changed.

Education and employment are in flux as they evolve to meet the needs of the next generation. Young people are looking at the world differently from the generations that came before them. In the midst of all these seismic shifts, how are parents, educators, employers, and communities preparing the kids of today for a strong future tomorrow?

As the workforce continues to reinvent itself, robust academic knowledge is important for every young person—but it's no longer the only thing they need. To thrive, young people must also possess both strong technical competencies and valuable professional (or soft) skills. It's a trifecta, and it's the new competitive advantage to empower them in their education and career journey.

As a generational expert, I deliver keynotes all over North America to share my perspective on this tri-faceted competitive advantage—and how we can help young people build it. I even wrote an award-winning book on this topic called *Answering Why: Unleashing Passion, Purpose, and Performance in the Younger Generations*. In this bestseller I call all of us to connect, engage, and answer why for the younger generations. If we can forge that vital human connection, we can inspire and equip them to embark on a successful career and life.

There's a motivational strategy I share with my audiences that I call "the Light at the End of the Tunnel." In this analogy, the Light is the reward—the goal, the thing you're striving for, and the Tunnel represents all the effort, time, and sacrifice necessary to reach your Light. Each person's Light is different because we all have a different picture of the life we want to live. The strategic component is how we as parents, educators, and employers are helping the next generation discover, embrace, and pursue their Light.

We must help them find their Light and then keep reminding them of it at every step of their time with us. They need to figuratively see, smell, taste, hear, and touch the Light to experience it in every way possible to stay motivated for their trek through that Tunnel.

Unfortunately, an alarming number of kids are standing still in the Tunnel. For a myriad of reasons, they're living in what I call "static purpose mode." They're passive when it comes to moving through the Tunnel. There's little or no forward progress.

What we need to do is help them transition out of static purpose mode into what I call "active purpose mode." Young people in active purpose mode see the Light and are steadily moving toward it. Their progress doesn't have to be fast, but there is progress. They take a step, and then a step, and then a step. All the while they are learning, discovering, growing— becoming. It's beautiful to see.

And the book that you're about to read is a catalyst to make all of this growing possible.

In this visionary work, Lane Walker grounds all of us in a simple truth: Through a meaningful human connection, I can make a tremendous difference in the life of a child. I can light their fire.

Today's students are remarkably talented, intelligent, and creative. They have incredible potential to make the world a better place; in fact, I believe they have it within themselves to become the next Greatest Generation. But for this to happen, caring parents, educators, coaches, counselors, and others must understand how they think and what makes them tick. Only then can we invest dynamically in these young people and ignite the spark of their greatest achievement.

*Light the Fire* is an important book for everyone to take to heart, because we all interact with young people in some way or another. Again and again, Lane reminds us of the intrinsic value of every child. For some children, lighting their fire is easy, while others require a tremendous amount of time, energy, and care to fan that flame. But every child is worth the investment.

Lane and I share the belief that every young person can and must be empowered in their education and career journey.

_Light the Fire_ connects to that bigger picture with highly practical strategies to engage with kids, build rapport, and become a role model they'll never forget.

The world is changing, but the power of forging a human connection is not. This book will light your fire to make a bigger difference for the young people you influence.

– Mark C. Perna
MarkCPerna.com

# INTRODUCTION

EVERY KID'S HEART constantly yearns to find someone who will listen, notice, and tell them how important they are to this world. It doesn't matter the age, socioeconomic background, culture or any other label you can think of.

I believe most people want to inspire and be impactful with kids; they simply don't know how. Maybe you have tried and failed. Maybe you are a struggling parent looking to connect with your daughter or a teacher struggling to be inspirational in your classroom or on the athletic field. Perhaps you are someone whose flame once burned so bright you could see it from space, but now you barely have a flicker.

This book could be the book you need to light your own fire, which will in turn help light the fire of some kids. This book is about making positive connections that will inspire and impact kids, and that small connection can help light the fire for much bigger accomplishments.

The past 20 years I have been a teacher, a principal, a mentor, and a coach. I have personally seen the chapters of this book come to life and be effective. I have lived these ideas and strategies. I know they will make an immediate tangible impact in a kid's life. This book was written for anyone who wants to be a difference-maker in a kid's life.

For the sake of clarity, in this book, the word *kid* is referring to anyone from kindergarten to a senior in high school. While some strategies do work even in adulthood, the focus of this book is directly on kids in the elementary age range through high school.

The stories in this book were learned through time and trial and error. After dedicating over half of my life to working with kids, I noticed that specific thoughts, ideas, and strategies had a direct, successful impact on kids.

Over the past 20 years, I have learned the secret to education: building a relationship with each kid.

I have dedicated my life to learning and pursuing ways to establish meaningful positive associations with kids. For the last 12 years I have been pursuing my passion as a principal and an educational leader. I love building a school culture that focuses primarily on investing and impacting kids.

My educational career started as a fifth-grade teacher. Then several years later, I moved and taught fourth grade. The entire time I taught, I was also coaching multiple ages and sports. My first administration job was as an elementary school principal, serving a K-6 building. Five years later I made the jump to the high-school setting, working as an assistant principal at a career technical center with high school students. Currently, I serve as a county career technical director and a principal.

I went from working with kindergartners to seniors in high school. High-school students are preparing to graduate and must make major decisions about their futures. When I made the career move from elementary-aged children to high schoolers, many asked if I worried about the challenge of working with older students and "bigger problems."

I soon realized that their problems and ambitions were the same as the younger children. Whether the kid is a kindergartner who can't tie his shoes or a high-school student who wants to drop out of school, all share the same wants and needs. Kids vary in size and age, but they all are looking for a connection. The heart of every child desires meaningful relationships.

*Do you see me?*
*Do you hear me?*
*Do I matter?*

They all ask the same burning questions that resonate in the soul of every child. Do you see me? Do you hear me? Do I matter?

Kids want to be noticed, they want to be engaged, they want someone to personally invest in them. They want to know that they matter and that someone (even if it's one person) authentically cares about them.

So notice what interests them in or changes in their appearance such as a different haircut, new glasses, a hobby. Ask questions: "How's the latest video game?" "Hunting?" "Fishing?" "Dirt Bikes?"

My passion for writing this book is simple: I want everyone who reads it to gain some simple, quick strategies and stories that will enhance his or her skill set. During my career, I have been blessed to learn from the best, teach the best and have the best case studies.

The following chapters will share practical, engaging ways to build positive relationships with kids that will have a lasting impact. Each chapter will conclude with a main point which summarizes the principal idea from the chapter. The "Main Point" will be followed by "The Big Three." These key points will provide quick, tangible thoughts, strategies, or ideas you can immediately apply on your quest to inspire kids.

For years, adults have been looking for a quick, easy way to connect with kids. They want to inspire and have an impact, but they simply don't know how. Or maybe they sincerely tried, and nothing seemed to work. Many adults are looking for a magic wand they can wave to connect with kids.

Guess what? There is no magic wand when it comes to inspiring and impacting kids. Rather, we need to shift our mindset, learning and using proven, effective strategies that will help make connections with kids. Focus less on the quick fix or the waving of a magical wand and set your goal to be a magician!

Are you ready to learn the tips and strategies to become a "kid magician"? You can be that person, my friend! You can light the fire that, with fanning, will burst into inspirational flames for kids.

This book is not a magic-wand fix for kids.

This book is designed to create magicians.

This book is all about investing and impacting kids—lighting some fires.

# 1
# LIGHT THE FIRE!

*Inspiring &*
*Impacting*
*Kids!*

"Education is not the filling
of a pail, but the lighting
of a fire."

– WILLIAM BUTLER YEATS

KIDS NEED YOU! In fact, they need you now more than at any other time in history.

Guess what? You need them too.

Culture and technology have changed at such a rapid pace that kids are being exposed to matters much earlier in life. They are losing their innocence and struggling with emotional issues tied directly to the Internet and social media. Their eyes and ears are constantly bombarded with edited pictures, captivating videos, and social media personalities pumping a false narrative.

This cultural shift kids are experiencing is dangerous and has made connecting with kids harder. It has given kids 24/7 access to anything they want at the push of a button. Instead of trusting a caring adult, kids are finding their meaning and answer to life by scrolling through their cell phone while isolated in their bedrooms.

Even with all the modern-day distractions and online opportunities, kids still need authentic adults in their life. They need someone who cares about them—someone who will listen and invest in them.

Our current generation of kids are amazing though adults might not always see or hear how great they are. Too often the negative is magnified. This group of kids, like generations of kids before them, will be successful. Their success simply looks different than it did when you were growing up. Think back to how different your childhood was compared to that of your parents. Huge technological and cultural changes were taking place, which made it hard for your parents to connect with you.

Even with all the variations in this generation, kids are still motivated by the same desire as our parents were all those years ago: they still crave a connection. They are constantly looking for an authentic adult who can and will make a positive impact in their lives.

Humans, especially kids, are ingrained for connection, and every kid is looking for connection. Every kid is looking for an adult to spark their relationship—to light their fire.

*Humans, especially kids, are engrained for connection.*

But how? What does that look like? It starts with a simple mindset—a belief that every kid matters. Lighting a kid's fire seems like an easy task; however, often it is not. Kids have fears, negative experiences, abuse, or other negative factors that prevent them from trusting adults.

So, the responsibility is on us—on adults who want to invest and make a positive impact in a kid's life. Win their heart, build a connection, and you will be amazed at the positive possibilities that can happen. If you start telling kids that they matter, they will start believing it!

Don't think that making connections and impacting kids is a one-way street. Making a positive difference in a kid's life is life-changing for both the kid and the adult who cares enough to make the connection.

This challenge to make a difference and light the fire comes with a strong warning. Make sure you are prepared and dedicated to the journey. Every child moves to the beat of his or her own drum and will require different levels of effort to spark the fire in his or her life. Some kids only need a daily hello or a smile, while others will require much time and effort.

You are providing the spark to build a relationship, create a bond, or simply be a positive influence in their life. When you light the fire, you are connecting with those kids, inspiring them, and being impactful. What does it look like to light the fire for some kids?

Picture the most gorgeous summer night you have ever seen. When you look up into the black sky, breath-taking stars fill the sky. The flashing pulse of fireflies fill the horizon with their blinking summer strobes.

A light breeze softly tickles your face, and the sounds and smells of summer are everywhere. It's the perfect night for a campfire. You take an old newspaper and some lighter fluid out to the firepit. The wood you plan to use is dry as it's been covered by a tarp to prevent water damage. The fuel is waiting for a spark.

The three pieces of pine logs are crisp, and the bark crackles, breaking in hand. You bend down slowly to add the wood to the firepit. After gathering up some additional bark and sticks, you add the newspaper and douse the pile with lighter fluid. Stepping back, you flick your wrist to strike a long match on the side of the box. As you toss the match into the firepit, a growing flame starts to engulf the fuel. Soon a huge fire engulfs the fuel.

That small spark lit the perfect fire. No other maintenance is needed; the elements were perfect, and the fire was primed and ready to burn bright.

Now imagine the same scenario, but this time it's been raining all day. The wood wasn't covered and is soaking wet. The sticks and bark are so wet they slip as you carry them. No stars are visible as you look up only to see a dark, bleak, black sky with no sparkle.

What happens when you throw the match in the fire? Nothing! The match burns for a second and fizzles out. Even after adding lighter fluid and another match, nothing catches. The wet fuel remains flame-free. The dousing from the rain has made starting the fire considerably harder but starting a fire with wet wood isn't impossible. New dry logs will be needed, and several additional, time-consuming steps are needed to light the wet fire. However, with some patience, more work, and new ideas, that same fire can be lit!

Kids are like both of these fires! Some kids are easy to invest in and need little-to-no extra attention. They are still looking for a caring adult, but they don't need the same amount of attention for an impact to be made. They still need you, but your investment is less. Their fire is far easier to light.

Some kids might possibly be aimlessly wedged between the two fires; the principles shared will help rekindle their fire.

The really difficult kids—the ones whose personal fire

has been soaked with water for so long it seems like it is impossible to light—are the ones whose spark constantly fizzles. No matter how helpful someone tries to be, their fire seemingly cannot be lit.

*Believe and see that the fire of really difficult kids is still worth lighting.*

In fact, many of these kids often spend most of their time trying to put out other kids' fires. The most important concept in sparking the fire is believing and seeing that the fire of these really difficult kids is still worth lighting.

No matter how much time or effort it takes to make a connection, every kid is worth it! Don't ever give up; kids need you! Kids need someone who will never give up on them and will always be in their corner.

If you refuse to give up on a kid, you can make a deep-rooted lasting difference in his or her life. It won't always be easy, and some kids will push you to your limits, but it will always be worth your effort. Not only will you be a life-changer, a motivator, a role model, and a rock star to a kid, but lighting a fire in the life of a kid will also change you in a positive way!

Are you ready to provide the spark that will light the fire and impact kids?

# 2

# IF YOU BUILD IT, THEY WILL COME

*Building
a
Powerful
Relationship*

"People don't care
how much you know, until
they know how much you care."

– JOHN MAXWELL

LIGHTING THE FIRE in a kid's life is dependent on forming a meaningful, healthy relationship. Developing a relationship is the most important act you can perform to be effectual in the life of a kid.

Relationships are paramount: they increase social emotional wellness, create stability, teach friendship, and build trust. Relationships also equip kids to handle adversity and challenges. Making connections causes kids to feel included and part of a community, a family and a team.

Rita Pierson was one of the greatest educators of our time. She worked in education for over 40 years and served in numerous roles, including elementary teacher, special education teacher, junior high teacher, counselor, assistant principal, director, testing coordinator, and consultant. Over the course of her career, she implemented and developed school involvement programs at large urban schools. Her life was dedicated to being the most impactful educator possible. She knew that how she lived and how she taught had a direct impact in a kid's life.

In 2013, Pierson died at the age of 61.

Her wisdom and legacy is timeless. As a result of all her years and accomplishments with working with children, Pierson believed the main key was making a connection by building a relationship with each child.

"Every child deserves a champion: an adult who will never give up on them, who understands the power of connection and insists they become the best they can possibly be,"[1] pointed out Pierson.

She recognized the power of relationships and the role they played in investing in kids. Such a heavy focus is placed on academic standards and testing. The importance of human connection—building a healthy relationship—should be the primary focus when you want to invest in kids.

Rita Pierson was a fire starter who worked tirelessly to light the fire of every kid with whom she came in contact. That relationship was her key to unlocking a kid's heart and eliminating barriers. Her conclusion remained the same her entire life.

Yale University professor, Dr. James Comer, said, "No significant learning occurs without a significant relationship."[2]

Money, power, and achievements all take a back seat to relationships. The most important feeling people want is love; we all want to love or be loved. How do we feel and show love? Through building meaningful relationships. It's the one and only way.

It's simple.

When you seek advice, to whom do you listen the most? From someone you don't know or from someone you love? We trust and appreciate the ones we love more than anyone else. We listen to them because we have built a relationship with them. The people we trust are trusted because they are proven. They have given their time, money, and attention; they made a personal investment in your life. Their words have the most meaning and sink the deepest in our souls. The people with whom we have the best relationships are the ones who listen, the ones who respond. And when they do, we listen.

Kids are no different.

Not only do they respect a relationship, but they also crave one. Their socioeconomic background, skin color or age doesn't matter; relationships are all that truly matter.

As a classroom teacher and coach, I found having a relationship was the key to the classroom or the field. Relationships eliminate problems and become the catalyst when problems arise. Trying to discipline or mentor a child before having a relationship simply doesn't work. All of these ideas in this book will be for nothing if you don't build a solid relationship. Kids will not respond or listen until they know you care and want to invest in them.

One of my favorite baseball movies is *Field of Dreams*. In the classic baseball movie, actor Kevin Costner plays a farmer named Ray Kinsella who starts to hear an audible voice coming from his Iowa cornfield. No one else around him can hear the voice—only Ray. As the film progresses, Ray meets a deceased baseball player named "Shoeless" Joe Jackson. Jackson was a former major league player who was infamous for his association in the "Chicago 8"—eight players who were accused of throwing the 1919 World Series in exchange for money. The eight men were banned from baseball for life. Ray had grown up listening to his dad tell stories about his hero, Shoeless Joe.

At the time of his father's death, Ray had been estranged

from him. This schism filled Ray with an abundance of regret. With the audible voice leading the way, Ray demolishes his farmland to build a baseball field in his cornfield. After building the baseball field, the voice returns, leading Ray around the country in a search for a 60s writer named Terence Mann.

Ray finds Mann who has now become a tired, worn-out, angry person who no longer writes or wants any ties to baseball. Mann has been drained by society and all its problems. The plot of the movie follows Ray as new challenges continue to come his way, constantly beating down his hope. On the brink of losing everything because he continues to listen to the voice, something in Ray's soul stirs every time he hears the voice.

During the climax of the movie, Shoeless Joe invites Mann into the corn and he accepts, disappearing between the rows, leaving behind an unhappy Ray. He had also wanted to be invited to go into the corn with Shoeless Joe and the rest of the former ball players. Mann disappears as Shoeless Joe stands on the pitching mound talking to Ray and his wife. Shoeless Joe turns to Ray and says, "If you build it, he will come."[3]

Confused, Ray stands thinking about what the former player had said. Suddenly, he turns toward the catcher who is slowly removing his gear. When he removes his catcher's mask, Ray recognizes his dad. The entire duration of the film, the voice had been leading Ray to his dad—to heal a broken relationship.

*Field of Dreams* focuses on the power of relationships and the natural void in a person's heart when a relationship is broken, or one simply doesn't exist.

The same can be said with our generation of kids: "If you build it, they will come." Spend time building a relationship, and the rest of the details will come.

Positive healthy relationships trump any new video game or the latest social media app.

Don't believe relationships are important? Imagine a funeral. When people are dying, they never talk about their achievements; all of those become meaningless. Instead, they talk about people and the relationships they have made. The loving people around them are all that really mattered.

Every positive interaction you have with a kid provides the building blocks to a healthy relationship. That intercommunication might be asking something simple about the latest video game, or talking about basketball, or having a jump rope contest. Converse and plan activities around their interests.

Being attentive to their interests raises accountability, and in the process, builds the relationship. I knew nothing about fashion shows and Barbie dolls, but after having three daughters, I consider myself an expert. I loved every minute of learning about their interests. As kids get older, I am learning that talking to them on their terms is better. I try to find places where I know they are comfortable and talk about topics I know they enjoy.

Try to notice every change from a new or different haircut, a brightly colored pair of eyeglasses, or a new sweatshirt. All are great opportunities to have a meaningful conversation with kids. Your noticing them tells them that you are generally interested in them.

Being involved and knowing their interests will pay big results as they become older. Take an interest in their choice of movies, the books they read, and their favorite television programs. Show them and you want to be with them and that you are interested in what interests them and what they like. Asking questions about characters and feelings will give you a good conversation piece into your child's heart. These kinds of discussions will also help them make moral decisions as they grow older. They won't be overexposed to inappropriate situations and circumstances if you are with them.

Kids will develop a moral code and know when something is inappropriate. Resist outside influences so you can ask authentic questions; they will know you are watching and observing even the little innuendos.

Have fun!

If you are dedicated to building a relationship, avoid actions and words that will tear it down. Embarrassing a kid or using sarcasm are wrecking balls when it comes to building relationships. Kids do like it when adults act silly. Don't be afraid to sing in the car, dance in class, or dress up on certain days. Kids love fun, and they are turned off to "boring."

Relationships are a blueprint for life that give us a firsthand experience of who we are and who we want to be. They also lay the early groundwork to be our true selves. Having an authentic healthy relationship with kids will help them deal with stress, have a positive effect on their overall health and teach them to feel compassion for other people.

# TIPS FOR BUILDING MEANINGFUL RELATIONSHIPS

## Make the time.

Plan time in your daily schedule that is not associated with work or academic matters. Try to have uninterrupted time to connect with your kids. These non-school-related subjects could range from their favorite animal to pizza. Value one-on-one time and use it with the kids who are having the most difficult time cultivating a relationship.

## Give them the opportunity to explain.

Asking questions is important, but make sure you give them adequate time to respond. Be careful not to inject your own opinion or experiences until they have finished talking. Allow kids to teach you—even if you already know what they are talking about. Kids have taught me about cars, dirt bikes, and manicures. They are passionate about what they are sharing with you, so listen and let them be the experts.

## Memorize it.

If a kid took the time to tell you a story, it's important. Make sure you remember exactly what that young person told you. That one time of sharing could lead to more meaningful follow-up conversations. Forgetting or restating the wrong information can hurt a relationship.

I like to research or expand on conversations with kids. When I go back to them with more information, their eyes light up. They know that I listened the first time and cared enough about them to dig a little deeper. This extra effort shows kids that you are caring and dependable.

## Celebrate differences.

Kids are unique and have a variety of different interests. One of the biggest hurdles in building relationships is the fact that we are all different. Kids feel much more comfortable when they feel accepted. Embrace differences! Don't let that any difference be a stumbling block when building relationships. Eliminate diversity as a stumbling block and celebrate differences and interest. Remember this world would be so dull if we were all the same. Kids have brilliant minds and see the world through a different lens.

## Let them have a voice.

Relationships are built on trust. Show kids you aren't threatened by sharing power with them. This tip doesn't mean you give your authority. An adult should never try to be a peer or allow a kid to be an adult. A clear role and guideline should always be established, but when you give kids a voice, what happens can be amazing. When kids feel valued and know that their opinion matters, they will respond; the relationship will flourish.

Kids often feel misunderstood or that no one really listens to them. While the distinction between an adult and kid is clear, they should always feel that you are giving them space to express their voice and be heard.

## MAIN POINT

*Positive relationships are the foundation
for inspiring and impacting kids.*

## THE BIG THREE

TIP #1

Be prepared to work. All relationships require a great deal of hard work and patience. Make sure they know you are in it for the long haul.

TIP #2

Relationships are always a two-way street. Even though you are in charge or someone in authority, respect must be mutual. Refuse to be offended by a child. Remember, they are still trying to find themselves.

TIP #3

Every interaction you have is either a building block or a sledgehammer. Words are powerful, so make sure you are building a foundation—not tearing it down.

# 3
# FOOTPRINTS OF HEROES

*Emulating
Qualities
of
Greatness*

"There is nothing in a
caterpillar that tells you
it's going to be a butterfly."

– BUCKMINSTER FULLER

WHEN I WAS a kid long before cable and satellite television, one of my favorite shows was *Mr. Rogers"*
*Neighborhood.* At our house, we only had access to three channels, and Public Broadcasting Service (PBS) was the only station featuring programming for kids in the morning. This lack of competition led me to turn the dial on our television set to channel 28 to watch Mr. Rogers every day.

When Mr. Rogers spoke, I really felt like I was his neighbor. There was no mistaking his empathetic, caring voice or his cardigan sweaters. He made me feel important and a part of his television community.

*Mr. Rogers' Neighborhood* aired from 1968 through 2001, and during those years, his message impacted millions of kids, including me. He taught us that feeling a certain way was acceptable, but those feelings weren't an excuse to misbehave. People are different, and that is okay. In fact, differences are beautiful and make the world a wonderful place!

Mr. Rogers had a passion to inspire and impact kids with a positive message. His agenda was clear, positive, and unbiased. His heart and mind truly understood how to inspire kids.

Fred Rogers said, "We live in a world in which we need to share responsibility. It's easy to say 'It's not my child, not my community, not my world, not my problem.' Then there are those who see the need and respond. I consider those people my heroes."[1] Kids need heroes—real-life heroes.

Mr. Roger's quote defines the responsibility we have as a society to help impact kids.

My life journey has given me a front row seat to observe, analyze and imitate some of the heroes to whom Mr. Rogers was referring. These lessons have come from teachers, preachers, custodians, bus drivers, parents, coaches, and other mentors. I have been blessed to have an educational career surrounded by people who maintained effectual relationships with kids. This career has allowed me to witness on a daily basis the traits and characteristics that have a direct, positive impact on kids.

These heroes have a number of qualities and traits that drive them. What defines them? They are life-changers. They have a heart to serve.

Kids return from college to have lunch with these types of people. They receive invitations to the weddings of their students. Some are coaches who receive random letters in the mail, outlining the impact they had decades earlier. They are parents whose children hug them and thank them for never giving up on them. Some are school bus drivers who smile everyday—exactly like they have for the past 30 years of driving the same bus.

These people are real-life heroes who have made it their life mission to motivate and inspire kids.

To emulate these heroes, you must be ready to follow in their footprints. You must be ready to recognize what makes these types of people so impactful.

To follow in someone's footsteps, you must see where those steps are and where they are going.

What makes these heroes' footprints so special?

Look at anything about which you are passionate and find the experts. Education isn't the only place. The sports world, business, entertainment, and industry all have their superstars.

Why do kids who have never seen Michael Jordan play emulate him on the playground or in their driveway?

Because he was the best.

Thankfully, I have seen some of the best—some of the greatest examples of adults who left a lasting impact on kids' lives.

As I have studied the educational heroes in my life, I have distilled five distinct qualities that stood out among the educational heroes in my life.

# PERSEVERANCE

All of the "great ones" owned and demonstrated perseverance on a daily basis. Perseverance is "the ability to never give up and to keep on going." Never giving up on a kid ignites a flame at the epicenter of his or her soul. Show every kid that no matter what happened today, tomorrow is a new day to be great.

Certainly, some days will seem like all hope is lost. If you are feeling the loss, imagine how the kid feels. To have an impact, you must model and teach that no matter what happened today, you start tomorrow with a clean slate. Children need to know that we will not give up on them today or tomorrow because we know they have great ability and potential.

The day an adult gives up on a kid is a dark day. Therefore, having a relentless attitude of hope and determination will make a huge impact with kids that will help prepare them for times when circumstances don't go their way. They will remember that you didn't pack it in or give up on them and that at least one caring adult is in their corner. Some might only have you! While that could be a huge weight on your shoulders, look at the kid's trust as an opportunity to be present and mindful.

Forgiving and forgetting their poor choices every day doesn't mean there aren't rules or consequences. Rather, the kids know they have someone in their corner who hasn't given up on them. Your continued perseverance and faith can make them believe they can be a doctor, a lawyer, or the next video game millionaire!

I learned the value of perseverance during my first year as a teacher. In my first teaching job I was assigned the fifth grade. I found fifth graders to be awesome, by the way. Such a fun age! A number of staff "warned" me about one particular student, whom I will call Sam. I was shocked by their warnings that made it seem like he would be an inconvenience in my classroom.

As I listened to Sam share some of his issues, I had the opposite reaction. In fact, he was one of the reasons I got into teaching and became a teacher who desired to inspire and impact kids—especially the ones that need it the most.

When the first day of school came, I was planned and ready. I spent hours upon hours planning the perfect first day for my first class. The day went well, but I have to admit that Sam kept me busy. He was a handful and needed constant attention.

For the next three months, I made building a relationship with Sam one of my main priorities, investing much time and energy in him. I knew all about his personal life, his pets and the newest video games he liked. I spent my lunch breaks sitting with Sam and throwing the football with him. I knew if I built a relationship with him, he would eventually come around.

The extra time I spent on Sam was worth it, and his behavior slowly started to improve. Then he had a rough day—I mean a really bad day.

His usual fidgetiness and outbursts were magnified for some reason. He showed an attitude, behaved rudely to the other kids, and spoke with a violent tone in his voice. He even swore, which he had never done in my class.

I had enough. His classmates had enough.

"Sam, please step out into the hallway." I didn't want to add to his anxiety or embarrass him, so I decided to call him outside of the classroom. I also wanted to eliminate his crowd.

When we were in the hall, I saw a fire in Sam's eyes that was burning brighter than other days. He was combative and rude to me—a behavior I had not experienced until this day. He yelled at me, swore, and stormed toward the main office, dropping several more expletives as he stormed away from me.

I stood watching in amazement, thinking, *this kid doesn't respect me even after all the time I have invested in him.*

The principal called his dad and sent him home.

I remember sitting at my desk after school full of negative emotions. I was angry, hurt, and upset that he had acted so disrespectful and had vented his frustrations on me in such an unhealthy way. That night I barely slept as hundreds of scenarios played through my mind. *The next day, I will be ready for him; he isn't going to disrespect my classroom and me!* My blood pressure was high, and my heart pounded. *How dare he act that way!* I tossed and turned all night barely sleeping. What a long, miserable night of my life!

I was so hurt and offended.

The next morning, I woke up stressed and ready for a battle. Not only had Sam taken away precious classroom time, now he was robbing me of sleep and enjoyment at home! My lack of sleep was obvious by the large bags under my eyes.

Not on my watch! I had done too much for Sam; I deserved better.

My heart pounded the entire way into school. I waited as the bell rang, smiling at my other students as they walked in. I could tell they were all wondering what I was going to do to teach Sam a lesson.

I looked across the hall and saw Sam fiddling with his locker. I felt my heart racing, my hands were sweaty, and I was ready to do battle. I pictured a modern-day Wild West shootout.

His head was down as he shut his locker and walked in my direction.

The entire class watched as I waited for him to say something rude to me as he walked in.

However, when he entered the classroom, his head seemed to be on a swivel. He was obviously looking for me!

He walked right up to me, looked me square in the eyes, and in a calm, empathetic voice, he said, "Good morning, Mr.

Walker." I saw no evidence of fire, hate, or anger. He was like a different kid.

I stood in shock.

No battle, no confrontation.

He had already moved on and had forgotten about yesterday. The tension left my body, and I stood there realizing what a fool I had been.

The rest of the year was great; in fact, he had an exceptional year. I learned that showing perseverance every day and starting anew was what Sam needed.

I learned to never hold a grudge and refuse to be offended by a kid.

A fifth grader taught me that I needed to show every single one of my students that no matter what happened yesterday, I am here for them today. I believe in them, and most importantly, I will NEVER give up on them!

## PATIENCE

Children need patient people in their lives. Personally, I struggle with patience on a daily basis, but I have learned that modeling and practicing patience can make the difference in the life of a kid. When I was younger, I was full of energy and inquisitive. I often forgot to raise my hand or even blurted out an answer. My mind raced from one topic to another. I struggled in a traditional classroom setting. I provided ample work for adults. Some took this challenge in stride while others often quickly grew tired of me. My parents made sure I wasn't a bad kid, but I proved to be a considerable amount of work. I remember Sunday school teachers who were full of grace and patience, their tone soft and forgiving, letting me feel comfortable and accepted.

But something powerful and life-changing happened to me when I was entering fourth grade. That change started when my mom and I attended my back-to-school open house. Up to that point, I was well known around the school as a kid who required a ton of time and attention. I knew I was an abundance of work. My mom knew it, and everyone around me knew it.

Some people tolerate kids like me, but the great ones love and embrace the type of student I was. That's when I met Mrs. Lukshaitis, a teacher who would forever change my life and the way I viewed education. That night during my back-to-school open house, she made one statement that would stay with me and change me. Her words and overall approach to a busy, loud, and hard-to-sit-still fourth grade boy lit my fire and fanned the glowing spark into a flame.

As we walked into my new classroom for the first time, I sauntered to the front row. Sure to find my name on one of four front row desks, I checked them all. After all, I always sat in the front or was moved there rather quickly. I was shocked when I didn't see my name on one of the front row seats, especially the desk directly in front of the teacher's desk. I attended a small rural school, and I had no doubt this teacher had already heard about me.

*Am I in the wrong class?* I continued to walk around the room, looking for my name and was shocked to find it near the middle of the classroom.

I quickly learned that year in school when I met Mrs. Lukshaitis was going to be different. Fortunately for me, she wasn't a typical fourth grade teacher.

She was unique in so many ways. Her outward appearance didn't match her heart and spirit. On the outside, she looked frail and weak. At this point in my life I learned that you truly can't judge a book by its cover.

Though she looked feeble and delicate, she wasn't. She was a lion in sheep's clothing! When she spoke, she was confident and firm. Her belief in kids and her passion for education roared on a daily basis.

She also had one of the coolest rides I had ever seen a teacher have. I can still hear the sound of her motorized scooter zooming around the classroom.

On our first day of class, she explained that she had the debilitating disease of multiple sclerosis (MS), and the scooter was the only way she was able to move. I heard no request for sympathy in her voice; she made it clear she was not a victim. Her scooter didn't confine her; it liberated her and allowed her to be active. She explained with grace and hope that MS had taken away her ability to walk.

I saw that she didn't feel sorry for herself and was full of life! I watched Mrs. Lukshaitis attack each day with positive energy and enthusiasm.

As my mom and I were looking at my desk, I heard the hum of her scooter and turned to see her smiling at me. She introduced herself, and I smiled. My mom started to tell her about how I was a good boy but was easily excited and had a hard time sitting still. Usually at this point, the teacher took the initiative to explain to me how important their classroom rules were and how I would need to be on my best behavior, and so forth.

I was shocked when she didn't. In fact, she didn't even let my mom finish her rundown of my outbursts and hyperactivity. Mrs. Lukshaitis interrupted her and said, "Boys are busy, and that's okay. I know all about Lane, and I am so excited to have him in my class. We are going to have a great year!"

*What?!* I remember thinking to myself, *What did she just say?* Her response totally took me off guard.

I saw that she was 100 percent genuine and authentic when she spoke to my mother with conviction and confidence. Her eyes and strong tone told me she meant what she said. I remember looking at her and believing every word she said.

That introduction was only the start of the lessons I would learn from Mrs. Lukshaitis. Every day she came with the same passion and enthusiasm for learning. Her classroom was exciting, and she was graceful, yet had high standards. She was not a pushover, but she listened. She had high expectations and kept kids accountable, but she knew about forgiveness and grace.

From then on, school took a different meaning in my life. I felt wanted. While I wasn't a perfect student, that year I started to learn how to harness and use my energy in a positive way.

That year I met Mrs. Lukshaitis changed my life.

She was one of the reasons I wanted to become a teacher. I wanted to be able to make students feel the way she had made me feel. Her patience made a connection with me that lit my fire for education. Her kindness had a direct correlation on my life-long desire and love of learning. She inspired me not to see the faults in kids, but to look for the uniqueness that makes each one great.

Our kids need people who are patient. Each child will have his or her own individual struggles, and some will be much more difficult than others. Both modeling and practicing patience is a great way to connect with a kid. As I became a teacher and eventually a principal, I always remembered the lesson a fourth-grade teacher modeled for me. I always tried to show kids grace and welcome them into my classroom each day. What happened the day before didn't matter. Every day was a fresh, new start, and every student was always welcome in my classroom.

## ATTITUDE

Attitude is a daily choice: it's that simple.

Every day you get to choose your attitude. In a world with several uncontrollable aspects, your attitude is one of the characteristics that you can directly control. There are no excuses. While influenced by your environment and the people around you, your attitude is yours to control and own.

Nothing you do on a daily basis will impact those around you more than the way you display your attitude. Both adults and kids will be directly affected by the way you see and react to life's situation on a daily basis. Do you bring an attitude of excitement and positivity to your home, classroom, or field of work? Or do you wear your emotions on your sleeves?

Like it or not, kids will feed off of your attitude.

Do you have a thankful, hopeful attitude?

Do you "get" to go work or "have" to go to work?

Do you "get" to go to your kid's baseball game? Or do you "have" to watch more baseball games?

"Getting" to go to work tells everyone around you that you love your career, you are thankful to attend to kids, and you plan to invest and serve people. "Having" to do a certain task tells people you would rather be doing other activities. "Having to" takes away from the value and the people involved. No one makes you go to work. Even if you don't like your job but need the money, you are still making a choice.

If given a choice, to which one would you be more attracted—the "have-to" attitude or the "get-to" attitude? Of course, the person who "gets" to go to work! People who are passionate and enjoy their careers spread that positive outlook through their attitude. Simply because some people might hate their jobs doesn't mean you have to!

The same idea is true with parenting—what a challenge! I am so grateful that I "get" to be a parent every day. I have never felt like I have *had* to parent; rather, being a parent is a gift for which I am so thankful. Don't let the negativity of others curtail your attitude.

Kids will observe tone and body language as they monitor your attitude every day. Choose to be positive and maintain an attitude of gratitude. Kids need to know you enjoy what you do and that you have the privilege of working with them. Your attitude tells them they are important, and someone is investing in them.

On a daily basis, I tried to instill two attitudes in my students: work hard and be nice. If every class member's general attitude in class was one of working hard and being kind, I knew we would have a successful school year.

Your attitude will have a direct impact daily, so choose your mindset wisely. The greatest inspirations in my life have had an attitude that reflected their love for being where they were. That love permeated through the person's voice and body language. They were fired up about what they did. They cared about who was affected. Their attitude reflected their passion for making an impact.

## UNBIASED

Want to take impacting kids to an unparalleled level of success? Be unbiased! Treat everyone around you with the same degree of compassion and love.

While implementing this attitude seems like an easy task, often it is not. The suspension of bias is often more difficult than you think. You will never be able to authentically work with kids until you can dismiss your own personal bias.

Resolving bias is vital. You must believe that any child is capable and able to learn and achieve great endeavors. To be fair, you need to look at each kid objectively. Kids need adults to make them feel safe and accepted. Unfortunately, bias has been around since the beginning of time. What a world we would have if every classroom, field, gym, and city were bias-free!

Every kid—no matter his or her ethnic background, socioeconomic status, or societal label—must be given the same energy and effort in order for them to learn and achieve like everyone else. What other people told you about them doesn't matter. Neither does having their dad in class 20 years ago matter.

Being unbiased is essential to capturing the heart of a child. Kids live with bias all the time, but when you are around, they should feel safe and not feel judged.

# ACCOUNTABILITY

The most effectual adults never make excuses or point the finger. They always look in the mirror and ask what they can do better. They own their actions and come up with a plan to improve the situation. They are accountable to themselves, their families, and the kids they serve.

When people value accountability, they own their words and actions. If something needs to get fixed, they fix it. They don't wait for someone to come along. Need money for an outstanding project at school? Accountable teachers search to find and write a grant to get the money. They don't blame poverty or a lack of funding as a hurdle to success. When you are accountable for your actions, you are the one responsible for them.

I remember hearing a story Rita Pierson, the exemplary educator, shared about accountability. One day she was teaching a math lesson on ratios. After teaching the lesson, she reviewed the teacher's edition of her textbook and realized she had taught the entire lesson wrong.

"I came back to class the next day and said, 'Look, guys,

I need to apologize. I taught the whole lesson wrong. I'm so sorry,' said Pierson. One child spoke up and said, 'That's okay, Mrs. Pierson. You were so excited, we just let you go!'"[2]

Dr. Pierson worked in school districts with numerous issues as well as poverty. She did not allow those negative elements to become barriers in her classroom. She possessed a gift, and she knew she was directly accountable for their futures. She knew the buck stopped with her. She was in control of making a positive impact in kids' lives. All the other factors were simply obstacles that they would have to overcome.

Rita Pierson was accountable for her students' education—not their parents, how much money they had the bank was not part of the equation, the color of their skin had no relevance nor was their educational level related. Her job was to be accountable to every student with whom she came in contact.

She went on to impact and change the lives of countless students because she held herself accountable for each student. She didn't make excuses; she simply and constantly started lighting fires by being accountable daily.

# MAIN POINT

*Kids need you! It doesn't matter if you don't think you know what to say or do. They need to know that you see the butterfly in them—even if they are still only a caterpillar.*

# THE BIG THREE

### TIP #1

We have a responsibility to invest in kids. Remember someone took the time to invest in you.

### TIP #2

*Getting* to work with kids works so much better than having to work with them.

### TIP #3

Never show bias and know that you are accountable for the way you treat and interact with kids.

# 4
# BRING THE H.E.A.T.

*Sharing
Hope,
Enthusiasm,
Attention
& Time*

"The most precious gift you can
give someone is the gift
of your time and attention."

– NICKY GUMBEL

AMERICAN BILLIONAIRE ENTREPRENEUR and television personality Mark Cuban said,

Time is the most valuable asset you don't own. You may or may not realize it yet, but how you use or don't use your time is going to be the best indication of where your future is going to take you.[1]

Your time is valuable.

Kids' time is valuable.

We are running out of time. Too many people wait for the right time to change or learn a new concept. Your reading this book tells me that you have decided the time has come in your life to learn more about how you can have a positive impact on kids.

It's time to bring the H.E.A.T!

If you truly want to impact and inspire a kid, I know of no quicker way than to bring the H.E.A.T. Bringing the H.E.A.T. will light the fire faster than any other strategy within this book. This principle also lays down four fundamental core values you will need before you start your magical journey.

H.E.A.T. is an acronym that lays the foundation and provides the needed ingredients to help light the fire. Want to impact kids? Be ready to dispense **Hope, Enthusiasm, Attention** and **Time.**

# H — HOPE

Having hope means believing life can be better. Hope is vital for kids, and having hope produces happier kids.

Hopeful kids achieve goals, build relationships, and resonate so much positive energy they attract other kids. We don't want hopelessness for any kid. A lack of hope leads to poor relationships, diminished effort, and a helpless feeling.

Working with children requires your having a hopeful attitude. No one spots a fake person better than a child! If you don't believe there is a better path for them, then neither will they.

Children deal with many devastating variables on a daily basis, and yes, even the best athlete and academic student experience hopelessness. Covid-19, divorce, death, violence, and failure are some of the many hope busters that children experience on a daily basis. Even though each day brings many negative, awful encounters in this world, there is always hope!

Hope can be taught and, even better, this optimistic state of mind can be learned!

Adults have daily opportunities to model hopefulness to kids. Too often we wait for a bad event to happen before we talk about hope. Hope needs to be part of your daily language—both verbal and body language. Instead of waiting to repair a problem, build hopefulness in everyday conversations with genuinely smiling, using direct eye contact, and employing a positive vocabulary.

Being positive can be a personal, daily challenge. After all, life is constantly throwing curveballs.

How do you respond when your food is late, or the waiter mishandles your order? How do you deal with "that" kid in your classroom about whom everyone warned you?

Are you up to the challenge? Can you dedicate your actions, thoughts, and words to be hopeful?

# E — ENTHUSIASM

I loved teaching fifth grade. What an awesome age for learning and development, plus the kids are so much fun to have in class! Teaching is a difficult profession, especially in your first three years of entering that field. Sometimes you feel like you are trying to drink out of a firehose and simply catching your breath is a huge challenge.

I learned two extremely valuable lessons during my first year. The first reality I learned was what an amazing responsibility I had as a teacher. The power and influence a teacher has is incredible. I had a daily opportunity to make a difference in a kid's life.

*Enthusiasm is contagious!*

I wanted to be the best, have the best class, and reach every kid. I wanted my class to be a life-changing place where each kid wanted to come.

In the classroom is where I learned to value my energy. I learned that my enthusiasm had the ability to change the entire lesson or day for one of my students. When my enthusiasm level was low, so were the results in my classroom. I saw a direct correlation between my level of enthusiasm and learning. *Enthusiasm is contagious!* Enthusiasm is easy to see, and every kid wants to be around someone with enthusiasm.

When I was teaching, I noticed that whenever I became excited about my lesson, so did my kids. Even the enthusiasm level of my less engaged students increased. Students went home and told their parents about how exciting the lesson was. Parents told me that their child actually *wanted* to come to school. The students were more energetic, and I also noticed that their self-confidence increased.

Kids don't like boring.

# A — ATTENTION

I wasn't engaged, I wasn't doing it right, I was exposed.

I was a channel surfer. I wasn't giving my daughter the attention she deserved. My five-year old daughter stood in the kitchen, wearing a mismatched outfit. "Daddy, how do I look?" she asked.

I quickly glanced over my shoulder and noticed she was wearing a cute, pink tutu that she often wore. I had seen the outfit a couple of dozen times.

"Nice, honey. You look so cute," I muttered as I went back to the football game on the television. I had glanced over long enough to see the tutu, but the fourth-down play screamed for my attention. My eyes went back to the football game.

There was a short, inaudible pause.

After a couple of seconds passed, I noticed she was still standing in the kitchen.

"No, Daddy, I asked you how do I look? Did you see my socks?" she asked.

I turned. "Honey, I said you look good. I like the pink tutu," I replied.

"But you didn't say anything about my socks," she quickly answered.

I then noticed a pair of the knee-high multicolored socks with matching sequined shoes. The longer I looked, the more I noticed how much time she had spent assembling her outfit.

A quick, subtle glance wasn't good enough for her. She wanted me to notice her, to see every detail of her outfit she had assembled to show off for her dad. She deserved more than a mere two-second glance. She wanted me to *really* see her and all of her effort of piecing together her outfit. She had taken a long time to get prepared, and all I had given her was a few uninterested seconds.

What she was really asking me was, "Dad, do you see how beautiful I am?"

And I had failed—miserably.

I had chosen a stupid football game over an ideal opportunity to encourage and tell my little girl how awesome her outfit was. I could have said, "You are the most amazing five-year-old in the world!"

She wasn't happy with my original answer because she knew I hadn't really looked. I didn't notice *everything*. She had spent precious time getting ready to impress her dad, and I blew my opportunity to make a difference.

We are only offered so many opportunities to build and

encourage children; therefore, we need to capitalize on every single one of them.

I chose to watch a football game instead of giving her the attention her young heart craved. Too often, our daily lives are so busy, we often overlook the small details.

But to children, the small things are the big things. This principle has nothing to do with age; even 18-year-old "kids" want to be noticed. All kids want another person to authentically see them.

What my daughter really wanted was for me to look at her, engage with her, and shift my focus directly to her. She wanted me to shut off the television and tune into her. Instead, all she got was a channel surfer—someone who looks for a second but isn't really interested.

Kids don't need channel surfers; they need dedicated, devoted fans. So often we DVR or set aside time to watch our favorite television shows or movies. Our focus is 100 percent on that show, and the rest of the world shuts down.

*Who is getting voted off? What happens to our favorite character?*

Why do we allow our minds to channel surf when the most important, relevant characters are right in front of us? No one spots a fake faster than a child! If you don't believe me, ask anyone who has ever been a substitute teacher in school. If you are well prepared and accountable, kids will notice. If kids feel ignored, they will notice and take advantage of the situation, turning the whole class into chaos within minutes.

Let me repeat, no one spots a fake faster than a child!

Why do we give them short glimpses of our attention only to turn it off and move on to something else? Nothing in this world is more inspirational and meaningful than investing positively in a child's life.

My daughter wanted my full attention; she wanted my time. When it comes to the gift of attention, nothing less than 100-percent effort works.

*Attention drives and motivates the actions of kids.*

What a wake-up call I received from my five-year-old daughter!

Kids are authentic and pure—the truest of pure critics left in the world.

Attention drives them; it motivates their actions.

T-I-M-E is the most important element you can give a child.

Kids have a quality of innocence—a miraculous way of knowing if someone is genuine. In my living room, I was hit in the face with a strong reality. At that moment, I was a fake—a lukewarm dad. I was a wannabe—a fraud. I was more interested in a game on television than really noticing the beauty my daughter was showing me.

You may be reading this and thinking, *That doesn't seem like a big deal.*

But I am here to tell you that every positive interaction you can have with a child is important.

Try looking at it this way: social media, the Internet and cell phones are a constant reminder of the power of interactions. Kids are bombarded with thousands of false expectations and negative comments on a daily basis.

No one could ever convince me or minimize the importance of every opportunity to make a positive investment in the memory bank of a child. The good news is, if you are like me and feel like you haven't always taken advantage of these daily opportunities, you still have hope.

Start today! Start the second you put this book down. Don't live in the past and overthink past experiences; rather, use them as a motivation to be more impactful the next opportunity you get. Don't let your past determine a child's future. Maybe you're a teacher who is worn down with all the paperwork and long hours. Perhaps this book will help light the fire for you again. The best time to start is now.

I didn't spend my whole life waiting to be a dad and to be a channel-surfer. I didn't wash dishes in college to become a teacher to have students go home feeling like they weren't important in my classroom.

Kids will never be inspired by a part-timer.

I want to be the best—the best to ever live, the best dad, and the best principal in the world!

Why?

Giving anything less than my best is to have failed at the greatest task God has given me.

There are no do overs, no magical time machines—only now! The good news is it's not too late; it can start right now.

What was my five-year old was really saying? "Daddy, forget about football, forget about money, and just see me!"

Working in public schools for over 20 years as a teacher, a coach, and a principal reinforced what I already knew. All kids want to be noticed and valued. You cannot fully invest in kids without showing them that they matter and have priority over all else in the world.

# T — TIME

Time is the most precious commodity on earth. You can't buy it and once you lose it, it's gone forever.

What will you do with the time you have with the kids in your life? Are you building them up? Do you enjoy being with them? Do they enjoy being with you?

Time is the most valuable asset anyone can offer another human being. No matter how much money or power you have, TIME affects everyone the same. Whether a parent, a teacher, a coach or a billionaire, we all share the same amount of time.

The key is what we do with that time.

As a former high school football coach, I learned early on in my career that every team has the same amount of time to prepare for a Friday night game. How the players use that time is crucial. The Super Bowl is played the first weekend in February. The amount of time each NFL team has each week through the month of February is the same. Each team has the exact number of months, days, hours, minutes, and seconds to practice and prepare to be the Super Bowl champions. Every precious second could make the difference between being a champion or a loser. But the great teams—the winning teams—make the most out of the time they have been given.

To grow and improve, they use every second, maximizing every drill and every practice possible to get to the top. No day is wasted! Every player is expected to grow and get better.

Like a winning NFL team, you too can make a difference! Choose to engage, to celebrate, to teach, to mold, and most importantly, to love. The world is cruel enough with the many distractions and negativity that tug at the heart of a child.

Time is the best investment you can ever make for a child. But make sure the time you are spending is authentic. Make certain you are listening…and that you look at the entire outfit!

# Main Point

*Be ready to bring the H.E.A.T.! When you show hope,*
*enthusiasm, attention and time, kids will respond.*

# The Big Three

### Tip #1

Making a difference in the life of a child starts with hope. Kids need to know that there is hope—no matter their situation.

### Tip #2

Enthusiasm is contagious and needs to be modeled. The "what" you want them to learn is directly affected by the "how" the lessons are taught or shown.

### Tip #3

Don't channel surf or look at your cell phone when kids are telling you about their weekend, favorite color or animal. Be attentive and focus on them; they are sharing with you because it matters to them!

# 5

# BE THE EAGLE
# & AVOID CHASING SNAKES

*Tips for Responding and Reacting to Negative People*

"Learning to rise above petty gossip and negative noise gives you more time to get to the important working of living a big, luscious life."

– ANN MARIE HOUGHTALING

TEACHING KIDS TO be resilient and ready to handle issues and problems is essential to inspiring happy, healthy kids. Our world is a negative place; in fact, humans are hard-wired to be negative. We are surrounded by negativity. Many people would rather see someone fail than succeed.

Psychologist Silvan Tomkins performed extensive research on the psychology of affects and authored four books about his findings. Focusing on why human beings act and respond in certain ways, Tomkins believed human beings have nine innate biologically based *affects*, including interest/excitement, enjoyment/joy, surprise/startle, distress/anguish, anger/rage, fear/terror, shame/humiliation, disgust, dissmell.[1] He described these *affects* as the responses that result from a certain experience.

> Affects are the inborn protocols that, when triggered, bring things to our attention and motivate us to act. Affects are not the same as emotion. A feeling plus memory of prior similar feelings is an emotion.[2]

The researcher paired each affect to illustrate opposite ends of the spectrum—a mild reaction or an intense response, i.e., excitement is far more intense than joy.

Of the nine affects, only two *(joy/excitement, interest/excitement)* are positive. One affect *(surprise/startle)* is neutral, as this emotion can have both a positive and negative affect. The remaining seven are negative affects.[3] The affect Tomkins named *dissmell/disgust* could be described as the feeling a person has when smelling a dirty diaper or a rotten potato.

His research points out that only 22 percent of a person's affects are positive. This percentage reveals that kids will experience a high amount of negativity in life. To combat this barrage of negativity, those who have influence over kids need to build them and help them develop ways to handle adversity. They need to learn how to be equipped when negativity comes their way.

One way we can help them learn these techniques is by sharing stories or giving examples of ways to handle difficulties. Dating back to the beginning of time, stories have held a powerful place in society and culture. Early caveman drawings tell a story, and the Bible is filled with parables and stories that people meditate on and reflect about daily.

Telling stories is a powerful way to teach kids.

Kids with grit are prepared and refuse to be offended by peers or other people. They have a different mindset.

Words are one of the strongest weapons that can be used against others. Teaching and modeling an attitude that refuses to be offended at someone's words is a character trait that should be instilled in every kid. Kids need to know how to handle negative people who can bring suffering in their life.

The following are two great stories to share with kids about handling adversity. Make these kinds of stories part of your daily conversations with kids. Many times a story can teach what our words of wisdom cannot. For example, the story of the eagle is a great illustration showing how to rise above criticism and negativity. Animal stories provide great fodder for teaching truths about life.

The animal world is full of predators and prey. Some animals have been gifted with certain characteristics allowing them to hide, hunt and protect themselves. We can learn much about life by observing the behavior of certain animals. For instance, we know that wolves have a pack mentality and hunt and defend themselves by sticking together and fighting together, which teaches that principle that we are always stronger when united together. But what can we learn from animals about dealing with negativity and harsh words?

# THE EAGLE

We need to challenge kids to be like the eagle. Few other birds are ever brave enough to challenge and attack an eagle, but even eagles have natural enemies. Eagles are some of the most powerful and majestic birds ever to roam the sky. Of the 60 species of eagles, only two can be found in the United States—bald eagles and golden eagles. The grip of an eagle is incredibly powerful and ten times stronger than that of a human. An eagle possesses keen eyesight, which is eight times stronger than ours. They are cunning, fierce, intelligent creatures. But they are also a perfect example of the right way to deal with negativity.

The crow isn't like most birds...and definitely not comparable to the eagle. A crow is a scavenger—an opportunist. They are one of the few birds willing to challenge an eagle to defend their feeding territories. Instead of flying away or trying to hide from the eagle, a crow will attack. They swarm and attack the eagle in multiple directions, dragging and pecking at the eagle. Their goal is to harass and bother the eagle so much that he will find another place to hunt food or build a nest.

What does the eagle do in return? Due to its lack of maneuverability in the air, the eagle doesn't fight back. The eagle would have great difficulty in defending itself against the quicker, smaller band of crows.

Therefore, the eagle makes a different decision. Instead of responding to the negative or to the birds attacking and harassing it, the eagle makes a much simpler choice. It flies higher. It raises up. The eagle opens its huge wings and uses its strength and power to fly higher in the sky.

The eagle chooses to ignore the constant pecking of the crow and simply flies to greater heights. As the eagle flies higher and higher, the available oxygen in the air decreases. While the eagle is made for this altitude, the crow isn't. By choosing to ignore the crow, the eagle soars to new and greater heights. The crow eventually struggles to breathe and leaves the eagle alone. Without any fighting or debating, the eagle wins by taking IT-SELF to new heights!

You seldom win an argument with someone who is negative, and that person will suck the life out of you. They often only hear what suits them and listen only long enough to respond with another negative. Kids must deal with negativity because other kids are often cruel.

Rising above negativity is a great skill to instill in kids. Kids also need to know that when they face a problem in their life, not dwelling on the matter is important. Kids need to know that they alone can control their thoughts and actions.

# THE SNAKE

Imagine you are on a mission trip in the heart of some remote forest in Africa. The group that you are with has spent two days hiking and traveling farther and farther away from civilization. You are hours away from any relatively developed town or city, and you haven't seen a road all day. You are in the heart of the jungle, cutting your way with machetes through underbrush as you head toward a small village. Suddenly, you catch a slight movement out of the corner of your eye.

Bam! You feel a sharp, pinching pain in your lower right leg just above your boot. You look down to see two small puncture wounds side by side. Blood is starting to pool slowly around the marks and drip down your leg.

You see a movement in the grass and realize that you have just been bitten by a rare and poisonous snake. Your heart starts pounding so fast that it feels like it is about to burst from your chest. Mere minutes separate you from life or death.

*You have two choices:*

1. You can give chase to the snake, pursuing it back into the undergrowth to kill it.

2. You can hurry to the medic who carries the antidote and treat the life-threatening bite.

If you choose to pursue the snake, each painful step and each second that passes pushes the venom through the bloodstream closer and closer to your heart…and a painful death. The pain and the anger you feel toward that deadly snake rages in your mind; you want to hurt what hurt you.

Would it really matter if you found the snake and killed it? Even if you found the snake and killed it, you would be dead. **NEVER CHASE THE SNAKE!**

This story aptly illustrates what happens when someone offends us. Some people spend their entire life chasing snake after snake until eventually the venom either kills them or turns their heart black.

By choosing to leave the snake and work on our own injuries, we are volitionally choosing not to let negativity or bad circumstances control our life. Choosing to forget the snake is choosing to address yourself.

Kids face battles with negativity every day. The battle is between other kids, adults, or even themselves; seemingly someone is always looking to break a kid down. Equipping kids to handle outside pressure isn't enough. Sometimes their toughest critic is the one they see in the mirror every morning. Negative self-talk can be the biggest enemy to a child's self-esteem.

Ever notice that our inner voice is nearly always negative, allowing doubt, fear, and shame to drive our self-esteem?

My friend, what you say does matter. The words you use can make a huge impact both positive and negatively on kids. Neuroscientist Andrew Newberg, M.D., and Professor Mark Robert Waldman wrote the book *Words Can Change Your*

*Brain: 12 Conversation Strategies to Build Trust, Resolve Conflict, and Increase Intimacy.* The two researchers examined the correlation between negativity and stress, explaining, "A single word has the power to influence the expression of genes that regulate physical and emotional stress."[4]

Negative thoughts produce stress chemicals in our brains that undermine the way we deal with people, causing emotional harm and damage to our relationships.

According to Newberg and Waldman, words have a direct correlation with our brain function. Positive words can alter and strengthen cognitive function, which promotes a positive resiliency within our brains. Hostile language has the same affect in a negative way. Research reveals that negative words increase the activity in the *amygdala*, the fear center of our brain. Indeed, words will have a direct correlation with a person's relationships and feelings.

Newberg and Waldman advise, "Choose your words wisely because they will influence your happiness, your relationship, and your personal wealth."[5]

One way to battle negativity is to teach kids to have an attitude of gratitude. Teaching kids to appreciate the good in their life allows them to value themselves and the people around them. This sense of gratitude leads to a higher level of optimism and happiness. Adults play a key role in nurturing positivity in the life of a kid.

A major way of helping kids grow and being the best they can be sometimes requires pointing out what they could do differently. Feedback is only given with the intent to help a kid's self-esteem—not damage it. Toxic or negative feedback can cause the *affect* of shame/humiliation to a kid.

Our job is to help kids grow in healthy ways. But negative, toxic people will find them, and even the strongest will struggle to battle their negative poison.

# SOME WAYS TO HELP KIDS SHIELD NEGATIVITY

## Share Authentic Feedback.

Encouraging kids to be who they are is so important. They should also be able to handle honest feedback. Keep the comments positive and let them know that their attitude toward something has a direct impact on the outcome. Negative thoughts produce negative results. Not all feedback can be positive but try to frame your observations to keep the conversation as positive as possible.

## Realize Other People Don't Determine Your Happiness.

Kids need to realize that most people will never know everything about them. When someone spouts some unkind words, in all likelihood, that person doesn't know how funny, caring, brave, and smart his "victim" is. They don't really know the *true* you. Kids need to understand that their happiness doesn't depend on what others think of them. A healthy self-esteem begins internally—within themselves. A kid's happiness should never depend on what others say or think.

## Stay Calm and Use Low Tones.

When children share about negativity in their life, stay calm and temper your voice. Never cause a kid to regret telling you something by overreacting or becoming angry or upset. Even though you might be burning up on the inside, don't show that emotion in front of them.

Kids don't want to have to worry about your reaction or feel anxiety or become apprehensive about how you will han-

*Promote the positives and avoid the negatives.*

dle whoever is bringing negative into their life. Showing negative emotions is easier, but in the case with children, avoid taking the easier way.

## Promote good news.

Whether in a classroom or the home setting, create positive ways to promote the good qualities in their life. Teach kids to use positive words and to talk and be transparent about their emotions. Try to find good news in newspapers, on the television, or on social media that promote the good in the world. Promote the positives and avoid the negatives surrounding them.

Maintain good eye contact and smile when discussing the day's events. Kids will perceive negativity in your voice, so slow down your speech and choose your positive words carefully.

The more good kids see and hear, the more good they will want to see. Encourage them to always look for the silver lining in situations and people. Equip them to handle negative people and allow them to distance themselves from negative thoughts and people. Negativity will come; absorbing the bad and becoming negative is far easier when surrounded by constant pessimism. Dealing with negative people doesn't have to be a roadblock. Kids need to develop their own thoughts and feelings strong enough to prevent negativity from piercing them.

## Main Point

*Teach kids to rise up like the eagle*
*and teach them never to chase the snake.*

## The Big Three

Tip #1

Embrace the eagle mindset! When negativity comes your way, wing your way to new heights where haters cannot go!

Tip #2

Winning an argument with a negative person usually doesn't happen; they are too concerned with responding.

Tip #3

If you are bitten by a poisonous person, address the wound, but never chase the snake!

# 6

# "CAN YOU HEAR ME NOW?"

*Applying the Art of Listening*

"Most people do not listen with the intent to understand; they listen with the intent to reply."

– STEPHEN COVEY

L ISTENING IS A skill and an art.

Early in my career as a principal, I realized I wasn't a good listener—not because I thought I knew the answers, but because I was a problem solver. I knew teachers came to me when they wanted help or when they had a tough decision to make. I always felt the need to interject or to find a solution to a problem instead of simply listening to what they were trying to say. I was so worried about replying I often didn't hear what the person was really trying to share.

Listening is one of the most important skills to teach a child. We spend years educating students on reading and writing, but one of the most important aspects of language—the art of listening—is often overlooked.

*Listening is key to building a strong, trusting relationship.*

Being a good listener isn't easy; in fact, listening to someone else's views can be quite uncomfortable. I believe that discomfort arises because we often don't know how to listen.

We tend to only hear what we want to hear. We often listen in order to reply or lecture, instead of listening to hear what the person is really saying.

Listening is the first step to problem solving. Listening is key to building a strong, trusting relationship. Kids are crying out for someone to hear them. However, hearing them cannot happen unless you close your mouth and open your ears.

The Greek philosopher Epictetus said, "We have two ears and one mouth so that we can listen twice as much as we speak."[1] Epictetus spent much of his youth as a slave in Rome, eventually gaining his freedom after the death of Nero. He obviously knew the power of being an active listener.

Although we often make a half-hearted attempt, we aren't *active* listeners. Outside influences like jobs and money, for example, run through our minds. As we listen indifferently to someone's conversation, we miss great opportunities—ones that can make an immediate impact.

When kids talk, stop and listen. What are they really trying to tell you? Listen with everything you have—not just with your ears but your eyes and heart. Adults tend to listen so they can advise, get their point across, or solve a problem. The person who listens to solve or advise isn't actually listening; rather, he or she is simply waiting for a break in conversation to reply.

Don't let your own thoughts stop them from communicating with you. When a child talks, he or she is honest. On the other hand, adults tend to filter what they are saying based on their past experiences. Your experiences might be a good reference, but first make sure you are hearing what they are trying to tell you. Active listening doesn't make you the judge or jury; rather, it shows that you really care about what matters the most—what your child is feeling.

Not all that a child tells you will involve a major event, but listening will still build trust. The more you listen, the more children will really open up to you. The more you listen, the more they will seek your counsel and advice.

## THE MORE YOU TRULY LISTEN, THE MORE THEY WILL TRUST YOU.

### Listening = Trust

Once trust is present in their relationships, kids open up and communicate in amazing ways. The lasting effects for failing to listen can be detrimental. This present generation of kids are crying out for someone to really hear them.

My friend, are you *really* listening?

Author Stephen Covey included a blueprint of what active listening looks like in his book, *The 7 Habits of Highly Effective People*. Covey outlined the importance of listening, the power of empathic listening, and what it really means to listen.

> When I say empathic listening, I mean listening with intent to understand. I mean seeking first to understand, to really understand. It's an entirely different paradigm. Empathic listening gets inside another person's frame of reference. You look out through it, you see the world the way they see the world, you understand their paradigm, you understand how they feel.[2]

Utilizing empathetic listening is both powerful and life-changing but requires the time and effort of a trusted, caring individual.

# The Dangers of Not Listening Are too High!

When kids conclude that no one is listening to them or hearing them, they feel lost and that no one cares. Kids often express themselves with signs and hints about life to the people who surround them.

My friend, don't overlook these signs! The price is far too high. We must stop and listen to our kids, or they will find someone else who will. In their youthfulness and loneliness, their choice might not be the best.

## Listening to Kids Makes Them More Likely to Listen to You.

Do you listen to people in your life who never listen to you? No, you listen to people who have been active listeners in your life—people you can trust and those you know who care. How did they earn that respect? Quite simply, they have listened to you in the past.

Kids are no different. If you truly want a child to listen to you, *you* must first become a listener. If you desire to be a person kids will follow and respect, listen to yourself. What kinds of words do you use? How do you speak to others? If you use negative words, your child will be much less likely to come to you for any advice or guidance. They hear all that you say, how you say it, and they will make judgments as a result of their listening.

## Being Both a Listener
## and a Lecturer Is Hard.

Lecturing will not help teach your child about listening. Indeed, adults want to share their wisdom with kids and keep them from making mistakes they may have made in their youth. Frankly, lecturing kids doesn't work. Lecturing kids often leaves them feeling bad, whereas listening allows them to have an active voice. When kids feel like they are being lectured, they tend to feel that they have fallen short of an adult's expectations.

Kids want engagement; they want to be heard before receiving feedback. When you ask engaging questions, children will respond. As they grow older and have to make tough decisions about serious issues, they will have to be much more open and more inclined to listen to your ideas—if you are a good listener first.

Kids are not you, so don't assume they think like you do. They have totally different feelings, and they are often searching for different answers. To be an excellent listener, you must focus on them and their needs. Lecturing doesn't foster responsibility. When working with kids, less is more. Allow them to do a majority of the talking. Kids aren't always looking for a solution or an answer to their problem. They often just want to be heard!

Best-selling author, Bryan H. McGill, said, "One of the sincerest forms of respect is actually listening to what another has to say."[3]

Being a good listener sounds easy, but often it is not. Sometimes listening can become uncomfortable when you hear words you don't want to hear. At these times your natural response to counter instead of listening will be triggered, and you must control yourself. Listening will allow kids to see you as an ally—not an enemy. How kids perceive you is a strong factor in building trust and will keep kids wanting to come talk to you.

# Be a Duck on the Water

Nothing will end a conversation faster with a kid than exhibiting bad body language. Being an active listener requires controlling your body language. Kids pick up on adult's nonverbal cues faster than the words he is saying. Body language will be the key determining factor in really listening to kids.

I try to apply the duck-on-the-water metaphor. Let me explain. Ever notice a duck swimming around on the water? They glide so smoothly with seemingly little-to-no effort. English actor Michael Caine said, "Be like a duck. Calm on the surface, but always paddling like the dickens underneath."[4] Try not to be surprised with what a kid tells you.

This skill has taken me years to try to perfect, and yet I still find I must remind myself about controlling my body language. When you are having a conversation with a kid, listen without showing emotions and try to keep your body language under control. Let them see the duck, calm and effortlessly paddling around the lake. Even though your mind might be kicking and moving, don't show it. Controlling your body language will go a long way when listening to a kid.

Listening to kids improves your interpersonal relationship and encourages them to listen to you. Your focused listening will increase their self-esteem and help develop real-world skills. Listening opens up lines of communication that leads to understanding. Avoid the temptation to fix their problems.

# TEN EFFECTIVE WAYS TO REALLY LISTEN TO KIDS

1. Stop talking and eliminate outside distractions; focus solely on them.

2. Look them straight in the eyes—no matter how short or tall they are.

3. Don't feel like you have to advise or lecture. The time for that comes when they are finished. Neither do you need to have a response ready to be a good listener.

4. Credit their feelings; don't try to discount what they are telling you.

5. If you are unsure of what they are saying, ask them to repeat it. Try to refrain from paraphrasing or repeating what you *think* you heard.

6. Look for other hints such as body language, attitude, and other nonverbal cues.

7. Repeat back what they are saying so you know exactly what they are trying to say.

——

8. Always stay positive and calm.

9. Never interrupt; let them share their entire message before responding.

10. No matter how you feel, always stay respectful.

Listening is a skill, an art form. The basic requirements of being patient, open-minded, and nonjudgmental requires our being quiet and not putting our words into kids' mouth. When you become a good listener for others, you will also become a good listener to yourself. Listening requires respect for both people—not only for the one who is talking. A good listener will make kids feel connected.

## Main Point

*When you become an active listener,*
*you will actually hear what a child is telling you.*

## The Big Three

Tip #1

Be an active listener. Make direct eye contact and listen with your heart. Even if you have an amazing point to make, listen and wait for the appropriate time to share.

Tip #2

You don't have to solve their problems every time! Sometimes they simply want to be heard and for you to know what is on their mind.

Tip #3

"One of the sincerest forms of respect is actually listening to what another has to say," Bryan H. McGill.[3] Never waste or pass up an opportunity to listen to a child.

# 7
# MIRROR, MIRROR ON THE WALL

*Making*
*Self-Confidence*
*a*
*Priority*

"A child's bucket of self-esteem
must be filled so high that
the rest of the world can't poke
enough holes to drain it dry."

– ALVIN PRICE

KIDS SEE A variety of characteristics when they look in the mirror. Their self-reflection has a huge impact on their self-confidence.

When kids feel self-confident, they are more likely to be successful. Being able to see value in themselves and trusting their abilities allows them to encounter challenges and cope when they make mistakes.

Never underestimate the importance of healthy self-confidence.

Having positive self-esteem helps them with social skills, builds resilience, creates positive problem-solving skills, and helps them reach their full potential.

A self-confident kid will trust his or her abilities, qualities, and decision-making. Healthy self-confidence gives kids a balanced view of themselves even when flaws are present. Self-confidence creates less fear and anxiety while driving them to embrace a stronger sense of who they are and who they are becoming. Self-confidence makes kids happier.

- ► What do you see when you look in the mirror?
- ► How do you feel about yourself?
- ► Been working out? Lost weight?
- ► What do you see in the mirror?

- ▶ Received an F on a test that you studied weeks for?

- ▶ What do you see in the mirror? A failure? A loser?

- ▶ Gone through a relationship that ended badly?

- ▶ What do you see in the mirror?

That mirror is not simply an outside measure of how we think we look or feel; it is also an inside one. Our own self-esteem dictates how we feel about ourselves.

Self-esteem is how we view ourselves and our worth.

A kid's self-esteem is fragile and ever-changing. Kids face trials and challenges that cause them to question themselves.

Positive self-esteem is a foundational skill essential to growth and happiness. Research professor Brené Brown said, "You cannot give your children what you do not have."[1] This statement is a great reminder to all adults that we must practice confidence, resiliency, perseverance, and kindness. When our weaknesses and doubts surface, our children will see them.

Kids live in a world dominated by social media and instant critique. Our job as adults is to do all that is possible to build a strong sense of self-esteem, value, and worth in kids.

Children with high self-esteem are happier and feel valued. They believe they matter and are important in the world.

Having self-esteem gives a child the courage to try new endeavors, meet new friends, and accept imperfection. When a new undertaking goes wrong, kids with self-esteem believe in themselves enough to try again. A good self-esteem enables kids to see the good in themselves, causing them to set goals and accept themselves—even when they make mistakes.

Kids who lack self-esteem are unsure and not as happy as those with a good self-esteem. They think they are not good enough or accepted. They may remember that one time they failed over the thousands of times they succeeded. Because of their fear of failure, they won't step out of their comfort zones. These kids have a hard time seeing any good in themselves.

Every child is a blessing and wonderfully made. They may not feel that way, but they are.

The world is a cruel place. Schools especially are a melting pot for all kinds of unkind attitudes and harsh judgments. What a tough environment for any kid! But for the kid who lacks self-esteem, school becomes an even tougher environment to thrive.

Kids especially need help to battle their self-esteem issues. I cannot stress the importance of helping kids develop a good self-esteem. Believing that every kid is priceless is the starting point for helping them.

The roughest, most hard-to-love kids are usually the ones who have a negative view of themselves. However, a low self-esteem is not limited to those "types" of kids. A lack of self-esteem can affect every kid from the class clown to the trouble-maker to the super athlete, to the valedictorian.

Kids want to know that they are capable and that someone believes in what they can be—even if they don't see it themselves. Promoting positive self-esteem allows children to know that everyone makes mistakes or has issues, but the key is to learn from them. Addressing the subject of self-esteem can be tough for adults. Negative self-talk and years of mistakes may have caused adults to question their own level of self-esteem.

In order to ignite and inspire kids, we need to show them that they can trust in themselves, rebound, and learn from failure. We need to help instill a positive, I-can-do-it attitude every time they look in a mirror or question themselves.

# WAYS FOR KIDS TO BUILD THEIR SELF-ESTEEM

**1. Adults need to model self-esteem themselves.** My friend, stay away from negative talk. Even though you have struggles, model your confidence, and believe in yourself. If your children grow up with a healthy self-esteem, the quest for one starts with you. When you have children in your care, the time has arrived for you to polish your own mirror and look at yourself in a positive way.

Children are the greatest translators. When adults radiate self-confidence and respect, they will see it and respond.

Always use positive self-talk. Our family has a rule; we do not ever use the word *"can't."* Starting early on, we adopted this principle that we continue to use today. The word is never heard in our house. If I hear the word being used, I quickly remind them, "We don't say *can't.*" Not using the word is a simple daily reminder to eliminate negative thoughts.

**2. Perseverance brings praise!** Be warm and responsive when a kid experiences a setback. Your attitude will set the stage for how they handle mistakes in the future. Teaching resilience and a relentless attitude sets each kid up for success. Kids simply cannot always see the big picture. Having a gentle, inviting attitude when a hurdle or an obstacle must be negotiated is key to building perseverance. Praising a child and giving positive feedback is key to success, but make sure your praise is authentic. Be realistic as you commend a child and make sure you are praising effort before outcome. Try to focus on small achievements before tackling some of the larger subjects.

**3. Become the passion police.** Every child has gifts and talents—even if he thinks otherwise. A kid who discovers his own identity has taken a huge step in developing his self-confidence. When he discovers his passion, encourage him to excel in that area. In all likelihood, he has discovered his talent.

Encourage kids to explore their interests and develop their sense of identity. Every child has at least one strong passion in this world that excites him. Help him discover that interest and then load him up with constant encouragement. For instance, if he loves American history, find a book he would enjoy reading.

Celebrate what a child does well and find ways to highlight what he does well. Maybe his passion is a passing fad you know very little about. If so, take the time to do some research. Be able to have an educated conversation about what makes that kid passionate about life.

Focus on a child's strength instead of his flaws. Build on what the kids are good at and encourage them to pursue that interest with passion.

**4. Failure is part of the growth process.** Whether in your house, on the football field or basketball court, or in your classroom, wanting the best for each kid is perfectly acceptable. Adults are ingrained to protect kids, and when adversity comes, the protection instinct is strong. Keep in mind that some of the best lessons a kid can learn is through failure. From trial and error, kids can learn to work harder and demonstrate a better effort by failing. Experiencing a lack of success will also help prepare children to become responsible adults. Challenges that kids face often leads them to success.

5. **Create unique jobs or goals.** Allow kids to take ownership in a job that makes them feel special. When I used to teach, I had special jobs for each student every day. At parent-teacher conferences, I would often have parents comment how they could never get "Junior" to work. What I found amazing was each child's special job was always completed and done with precision.

Why? Because the jobs were meaningful, and the kids took great pride in helping their peers. This trip can apply to classrooms, the sports field, and at home. Make the jobs meaningful and something important to other people. Make the job fun, call the jobs by cool nicknames, and show the worth behind each job. Giving children jobs tells them that they are trusted. If you trust them, kids will start trusting themselves. Help kids set goals that are managed and focused on improving their weaknesses.

6. **There is no such thing as perfect.** Kids struggle when they make mistakes. Even though these mistakes happen, too often kids erroneously believe they have to be perfect. Having high expectations is fantastic; in fact, I have an entire section designated to that subject later in the book. I want to be

clear: being perfect is *not* the same as having high expectations. When a child thinks everything needs to be perfect, they will never be happy or satisfied. Even when a perfectionist succeeds, that person is having a hard time enjoying his or her accomplishment. Perfectionism leads to elevated anxiety, being overly sensitive, and being critical of themselves and others. All of these factors lead to a higher level of stress.

Growing up is stressful enough; kids shouldn't have to battle perfectionism. Adding a healthy self-image can thwart the need to be a perfectionist. Set realistic goals and expectations, talk about failure, share past experiences, and model healthy self-talk.

7. **YOU MATTER!** Every kid wants to feel that he belongs or is accepted. Kids need to hear that they add value to your life and that they matter to you. Once a kid realizes that you care, you feel he is important, he will achieve unbelievable goals. Make kids feel like they are an integral part of something bigger—an essential part of the family.

This point applies to school and sports. Build a family atmosphere where each child feels important and like a vital part of the team. Doing so allows kids with the ability to get and give love. Kids learn to care about their peers as well as themselves. They want to start coming to class and are less likely to skip practice when they know a caring adult is there waiting to see them.

To build self-esteem, the emphasis needs to be put on them. Instead of saying "I," use the word "you." For example, instead of saying, "I love the way you colored that picture!" try saying something like, "You took your time and made an amazing picture." When we start with *you,* they can see they are the direct result of the good that happened. Saying "you" goes much further than simply saying "Good job!" and places all the emphasis on what the child did. This simple change in verbiage shifts and boosts self-confidence.

The following are some concise tips easily remembered to utilize when trying to build self-confidence in kids.

- ▶ Avoid comparing kids to each other.
- ▶ Develop realistic exceptions.
- ▶ Try to provide choices to give them a voice in any decision.
- ▶ Focus on strengths instead of weaknesses.
- ▶ Never use sarcasm! It doesn't work, and it hurts.
- ▶ Don't judge; just listen.
- ▶ Forgive and forget.
- ▶ Respect their feelings.

Investing in a child's self-esteem is an investment in their worth. When kids feel more confident, they are more likely to succeed in life. Having a strong sense of self-esteem will allow them to handle failure, confront problems, and be resilient.

# Main Point

*Having a positive self-confidence allows kids
to value themselves and know they are important in the world.*

# The Big Three

### Tip #1

Kids with a positive self-esteem possess courage, make friends, and know good outcomes will happen. Having a positive self-image allows them to see the good in themselves and others.

### Tip #2

To be able to teach self-esteem, we need to model our self-respect! Our everyday language and attitude will have a direct reflection on a child's self-esteem.

### Tip #3

Instead of using "I" statements, substitute the word "you" in place, thereby shifting the emphasis of your feelings and showing kids you recognize that *they* did it.

# 8

# NOT EVERYONE GETS A BLUE RIBBON

*Cultivating a Winning Mindset*

"If you don't invest very much, then defeat doesn't hurt very much and winning is not very exciting."

– DICK VERMEIL

MAKE NO MISTAKE; life is about both winning and losing.

Before you write me some nasty email or leave a negative comment on Facebook, STOP! Keep reading and give me the courtesy of explaining.

What does it really mean to win? Winning simply means trying your best and never giving up! Losing is when no effort is put in or a person gives up.

Losing is when you quit.

I need to explain certain components so I can get to the root of what I am teaching in this chapter.

Recently, a major shift has taken place in our culture in regard to winning. Participation trophies and an idea that no matter what you do, you are a winner, is becoming more and more common. In most cases, trophies and awards should be earned. An earned trophy or medal will increase motivation.

It's dangerous to tell everyone, "You won; the outcome doesn't matter because everyone is a winner." I must ask, "Where is the reward for winning?" Where is the reward for the person who dedicated hours and hours to achieving the win? The dedicated person was awarded the same reward as the apathetic, indifferent person who did slightly extra and sacrificed little for the reward.

Depending on age and ability, I do believe times occur when kids should feel like their award or reward was winning. I believe this is especially true in younger ages, especially with skill-based sports. By no means am I saying that participation awards should never happen. I am saying to be careful—be very careful of what message you are trying to teach kids.

Giving every kid a blue ribbon is a dangerous practice. The idea behind "winning" is actually competing and doing your absolute best. To do that, the players practice and make trying to win a priority. If a kid does that, then they win; the score of a game or a test score doesn't determine if they won or lost.

Winning is about the effort and attention the kids give to be the best that they can be. If you do all that is possible and still lose, then on the larger scale, you really didn't lose! Losing doesn't always mean *failure*. Kids need to learn the only time they fail is when they quit trying. Self-esteem and praise need to be based on effort—not on outcome.

Taking a huge math test on Friday? What will you do from now until Friday to "win"? If you study for an hour on Monday night, never study the material again, and earn a C, then you didn't win. However, the kid who studies relentlessly for an hour on Monday, makes it his priority to do well on the test by reviewing the material on Tuesday through Thursday, and still earns a C, has won.

Don't think I am this overzealous former coach who only cares about winning the game. Such is not the case! I am far more interested in winning in life. Teaching kids to have an attitude to win every day is vitally important.

I believe some dangers can arise in teaching kids about winning. Social media is full of videos of adults who have taken winning too far. I have heard horror stories about coaches who are willing to cheat and lie in order to win—regardless of the price to be paid, usually by the players. Some coaches take undue advantage of kids and push them, causing them to hate a sport or a class they always loved.

In the end, the coach or the teacher who trains kids to win by game standards has failed those given into his care. Teaching kids that the only way they are winners is to become state champions is not a winning mindset.

I would be the first to say that kids need to know that winning is important! The goal should always be to win, but that intention doesn't always mean they are first or have the highest score. Kids need to learn to develop a healthy winning mindset.

Never minimize winning and make it what it isn't. If you are someone who tells kids that winning isn't everything, I hope this chapter makes you reconsider that mindset. Life is about winning. A kid will compete for a job, a scholarship, and his or her future spouse.

Teach kids to have the desire and the will to win the right way. Winning happens through selflessness and hard work.

Winning in itself is a choice and not always the final outcome. Having a will to win is what makes someone a winner. Kids need to learn that competition is healthy and an integral part of life.

The will to win should be a life-long goal that should be addressed. My friend, please don't dull down what it takes to win;

teach kids that winning does not come without hard work, discipline, and even adversity.

While teaching kids to be competitive and hardworking is important, don't make them think they are winners when they aren't. Not every kid will win first place; not everyone will win the blue ribbon.

Society wants us to teach our children that everyone wins, and everyone deserves a trophy in the end. This mentality is slowly killing the will to compete in our nation's children. We want them to feel good all the time and never have their feelings hurt. At a Little League baseball game, I once heard someone scream, "The score doesn't matter!"

*Oh, really?* Then why are we keeping it? How do you know who wins the game without keeping score?

Taking it a step further, aren't salaries competed for by the best and the brightest able to change their life through a winning mindset? Teaching kids that everyone is a winner demonstrates the philosophy that no matter how hard they work, it doesn't matter.

The philosophy that "Everyone wins" teaches kids that effort doesn't matter. What about the kid who spends hours practicing his jump shot to hit the game winner? What does "Everyone wins" teach them? The hours they spend working on their jump shot will increase their odds of hitting the shot with the game on the line. Missing the basket does not mean the player didn't do enough, and his work was in vain.

Someday, each kid will interview and compete for a job. They will go into the work force or to college, and some colleges and universities with limited enrollments require prospective students to compete for entrance into their institution. Employers are looking for people who value their job, put forth effort, and possess a winning mindset.

Those seeking a job will be either be hired or left jobless, but they won't get the job because they interviewed. Do you think they get the job because the employer doesn't want to hurt their feelings? That employer might consider their feelings after they have worked there for a few years.

Failures or losing is part of life, and often failure leads to our greatest accomplishments. Explain to kids that failing doesn't make them a loser. Failure is simply a part of life. How they respond to failure is what will determine their outcome. Talking about your own personal trials and errors shows them how you grew through your greatest failures.

The following list of some famous failures demonstrates the importance of learning from failure.

## FAMOUS FAILURES

▶ Michael Jordan, probably the greatest basketball player of all time, was cut from his high school basketball team.

▶ Elvis Presley failed music classes and was told he should stop trying to sing.

▶ Stephen King's novel *Carrie* was rejected 30 times.

▶ Abraham Lincoln wasn't elected to the Illinois Senate, but two years later he was elected the President of the United States.

▶ George Lucas was turned down by Disney, United Artists, and Universal before Fox agreed to fund *Star Wars.*

▶ Walt Disney worked for a newspaper company and was fired by the editor for lacking creativity.

▶ Jack Canfield wrote *Chicken Soup for the Soul* and was turned down by 144 publishers. *The Chicken Soup for the Soul* book series has sold over 110 million copies.

▶ Dallas Mavericks owner and billionaire, Mark Cuban, failed at almost every job he had before starting CompuServe.

▶ Media mogul, Oprah Winfrey, was fired from her first job as a television news anchor because they thought she was too emotionally invested in her stories.[1]

Can you imagine what it was like when you had to hunt and even fight for your dinner? Do you think clans would give their leader a high five for returning home empty-handed? Of course not! So why are we teaching our future leaders that everyone is winner? They aren't. One clan eats while the other starves to death.

Like it or not, competition has been here since time began. Based on achievements and performance, the smartest students are accepted by the best colleges. The best employees receive the promotions. The best athletes receive the biggest contracts.

Kids are living in the most competitive contest of all called life. Let's teach that effort and never giving up defines if they win or lose. Discuss how failure is part of the process—not a defining moment.

## PRAISE EFFORT—NOT OUTCOME

Kids need to know they are winners through their effort—not the end result!

In my years of serving as a coach, we had times when we lost. We lost because the other team was better than we were. Plain and simple, the other team prepared better, had superior athletes, and the coach outcoached us. I know of no fancy way to say it. We could have played that team 100 times, and they probably would have beat us every time. Eventually, even the best teams run into a better one.

When you praise effort, you have a concrete quality to evaluate. By praising the effort, even when you lose, learning occurs.

Did you know one size doesn't fit all with kids?

When you praise effort, you are judging kids on what truly matters, i.e., how hard they try. Their effort dictates your praise. That way even when you lose, or it doesn't go your way, effort is the one constant that a person can always have.

Having children is the greatest gift God can give a human being. I love being a dad. Having three daughters and a son is my highest honor. Even though all four of our kids were raised in the same house with the same rules, they each have their own wonderful personality. While each one has different strengths and weaknesses, the effort they put in is uniquely their own.

But during any given happening, sporting event, homework assignment, or daily task, they can be taught to do their best and to give their best effort. This skill should be taught and modeled.

► Will he win the spelling bee?

► Will he take first place at the science fair?

► Will he win every game in which he plays?

► Will he take the first chair in the band?

At some point, every kid loses in some way. Can every kid try his best every time? Yes! And if he does that, then he is truly learning the value of winning and losing. When you praise his effort, it's not about winning and losing; it's about his giving 100-percent effort.

Instilling that mindset in a child will carry over into school, other activities, and someday into the job field. Lace up your shoes, go out, and give all you have for giving all is what winning looks like. That attitude will prepare our children to be true champions!

Your child might not have the athletic skill to be the next Heisman trophy winner or possess the knowledge to win a Nobel Peace prize, but he can surely compete like one!

## MAIN POINT

*Winning is about the time and effort;
it's not always in the outcome. Define winning
and talk about what happens when you don't win.*

## THE BIG THREE

### TIP #1

Kids should have a desire to compete and try to win! Always put the emphasis on effort.

### TIP #2

Make sure praise is authentic and warranted. Be careful about overpraising common tasks kids should perform every day. There is a difference between achievement and common daily expectations.

### TIP #3

Put a high value on good sportsmanship. Make sure your child knows how to win with class and lose with class.

# 9

# ARE YOU A LAMPSHADE OR A LIGHTHOUSE?

*Developing
the Power
of
Positivity*

"When you see the good,
look for the good, expect the good.
You find the good
and the good finds you."

– JON GORDON

ONE of the most powerful tools you can teach kids is the power of positivity.

Want to see a kid be successful? Want to develop a leader, a future CEO, or a lawyer? Teach them to have a positive attitude. Inspire them to look for the good and be positive every day. How they look at each day will have a direct reflection of how people will view them and whether or not people will follow them. Every person can only make one of two choices: live positive or live negative—but not both.

There is great power in positivity.

We can either smile or frown, be happy or sad. Making this important choice will govern our entire day and have an immediate impact on everyone around us—especially our kids.

Make no mistake; being positive is a daily choice. Every day you have an opportunity to either shine a light or hide it. Some days will be much more difficult than others. Those really hard days are the days when you will need a positive mindset the most. No other choice will have a greater impact on your day.

When it comes to your daily attitude, you have a clear choice to be a *lighthouse* or a *lampshade*. Modeling positivity, which is the best way to raise positive kids, starts with you. Being positive might well be the hardest task you do every day.

Kids will observe two qualities in the adults working with

them. Your daily attitude will reflect how you see each day. You will either be a lampshade or a lighthouse, but you cannot be both.

What kind of a person are you?

# A LAMPSHADE

What does it mean to be a *lampshade*? Before sharing what I believe a person with a lampshade personality looks like, let me share the function of a lampshade.

A lampshade has a specific purpose of directing and filtering light. Its function is to control and filter bright light—dimming and directing the path of that light. A shade prohibits artificial light from shining as bright as it can, actually preventing light from reaching its full potential.

People tend to act like lampshades, and society, in general, is filled with people who tend to be lampshades, dimming or controlling the passion and excitement within kids. When you are a lampshade, a kid's true potential is manipulated and weakened. Having a lampshade mindset is an easy, lazy way to work with kids.

Lampshades are waiting to be offended. Social media gives everyone an avenue to express themselves, and when you add in the daily grind and difficulties of life, lampshades personalities seem to be everywhere. Instead of being happy for others, they find a reason to be upset, angry, or offended. Someone gets a new, higher-paying job, starts going to the gym, or buys a new vehicle, and they instantly go into lampshade mode. They get jealous, and their feathers are ruffled even though the person's situation has nothing to do with them. They always have words to say and most of the time it's negative or a complaint.

Often, their first response in the school arena to a change in a student's outside world is to judge, criticize, and control. They want to dictate how that student's light shines.

Their attitude tries to block people's shine—to shade them from positivity. Lampshades are the first to complain and the last to help out. They want changes in their lives but expect everyone else to make the changes for them.

Do you think anyone is attracted to a lampshade?

Are you? A kid will not want to build a relationship with a lampshade personality. Kids aren't drawn to lampshades, they won't trust lampshades, and they won't follow lampshades. Lampshades aren't inspiring or impactful.

Kids want and need to surround themselves with positive people—people who shine light into their life. Even as adults, we still have that basic need and desire to surround ourselves with positive people. As a child grows, he will respect and admire the ones who smile and never have a bad day because children are looking for lighthouses—not lampshades.

# A LIGHTHOUSE

Lighthouses were designed for one simple purpose—to protect and shine as bright as possible! A lighthouse beacon shines in all directions; the darker the night or more violent the storm, the brighter the lighthouse shines because of its purpose—to guide and protect. Even when treacherous waves and life-threatening fog moves in, the lighthouse remains steadfast and firm.

For sailors and boaters, a lighthouse serves as a strong tower—a beacon of hope. The light projected from the lighthouse guides ships and boats away from dangerous rocks and reefs—hazards that would that sink most sailing vessels.

A lighthouse saves lives while lampshades worry about themselves. Given enough time, lampshades will eventually suck all the light out of everyone around them.

A lighthouse magnifies light, using special crafted lenses to focus a concentrated beam of light that spreads and can be seen for miles. In the same way, the kind of person who attracts kids looks at them through special lenses—what some call rose-colored glasses—and magnify their positives and promotes all the great qualities about each kid.

Think about a person who has made a powerful impact on your life. You looked up to this person—perhaps a teacher, a coach, or a family member. I guarantee if you consider that person, he or she was a lighthouse. Maybe you had a coach who pushed you and helped you accomplish amazing achievements. Perhaps you had a teacher who stayed after school with you to work on fractions until you really "got" the concept. I call these rare people heroes because they made an impact on your life; they were lighthouses.

Every day you have a choice to make. You will either be a lighthouse or a lampshade, and trust me, you cannot be both.

Being a lighthouse for kids would seem like an easy task, but often the process is long and exhausting. One negative interaction can ruin a relationship with a child. One bad day with a lampshade mindset could do more damage than a hundred days of being a lighthouse.

At school, we try to have five positive interactions to every negative. That 5 to 1 ratio might seem high, but it's not. Social media has now provided an easy way for kids to be incredibly rude to each other. The buzzword *bully* that is bandied about in schools and in today's society has been caused by lampshade parents and adults.

Bullies have been around since the beginning of time. I believe they are the ultimate example of a lampshade. Society teaches them that being a lampshade is easier than being a lighthouse. But when you look deeper, this attitude of discontentment is being modeled for them. Bullying has become the scapegoat—the big problem in this generation. Why? Because that's what the adults around them model.

Simply put, if you want to have nice kids who treat others with respect, model it for them, show them how to treat people the right way. Be nice! Handle problems with a smile!

Kids will turn into lampshades because they are surrounded by lampshades.

How do you react when you have a long wait at a restaurant? What happens when the waiter or waitress make a mistake? How do you respond when your team loses or a bad call is made in the game?

Do you smile and accept the situation? Or do you criticize and cast stones? Kids will learn how to handle conflict by the way that you handle conflict. Every time you belittle someone or treat a person disrespectfully, you are teaching the next generation how to act.

How can adults get upset with kids for being negative when they are simply behaving the way they were taught? Being rude or making excuses becomes easy and even acceptable because that type of behavior has become a natural reaction to a negative situation.

What do you think the first reaction a kid will have when he becomes jealous or angry? They will morph into full lampshade mode.

My friend, this lampshade behavior starts at the top—with you! Therefore, you need to model the qualities of a lighthouse that doesn't bend or sway in the storm; it shines brighter. The darker the night, the brighter the light. Shining as a lighthouse might mean smiling even though your steak has been prepared "medium" instead of "medium rare."

My greatest interactions as a teacher came from being a lighthouse. Every year, usually at the end of the year, students would write me letters that I have kept and filed. I knew lampshades would come again, and I wanted to have something to remind me of my true mission. I love these letters, and I have always cherished them.

One letter in particular that struck a chord in my heart still stands out to me to this day. I use the words in that letter to guide me every day. A student wrote about how much he enjoyed my fifth-grade classroom, how safe he felt and how he knew I cared about him. He ended his letter by saying, "What I loved about you is that you never had a bad day!"

I remember reading that closing statement and becoming emotional because I know I had a plethora of bad days.

During that time, my wife and I welcomed our first children. We were blessed with twins—two wonderful girls. Even though we had many late nights, I loved every minute of it. We often slept three hours a night, and I lived off caffeine. I know I was exhausted; I just didn't let the students see my fatigue.

That's the trick! When you work with kids, you become great actors or actresses. We smile even when we aren't happy; we build even though we might be down. Every day starts and ends with a smile. We cannot let our bad days affect our students, athletes, or kids. If we want to make a positive impact in the life of a child, we must choose to be a lighthouse every day.

Lighthouses make an impact!

Those who are lighthouses will be the first ones to whom the kids will talk to and confide in. They feel safe because they respect lighthouse people. When conflict arises, being a lighthouse will allow you to have the greatest impact.

How do you impact change or give advice to kids without offending them? I consistently work with people who struggle with saying what they really want to say. They are either overly aggressive or too passive, and they end up pushing away the kids. They slowly turn into a lampshade without even knowing it.

Lighthouse personalities build kids. They know how to approach a tough conversation without getting angry, and they know how to get results. Personally, I found that incorporating the *Sandwich Method* had extremely successful outcomes.

## USE THE SANDWICH METHOD

Do you struggle with having authentic conversations that promote a positive change in a kid? Do kids think you are critical or trying to critique all they do wrong? Do you struggle with giving your point of view without offending a kid? Take a deep breath because you are not alone. In fact, the majority of adults have a difficult time influencing kids to change.

How do you discuss what really matters without slamming a door in a kid's face? I have always tried to use a technique called the sandwich method.

In my first year of teaching, I learned the power of *compliments versus complaints*. I quickly discovered that kids and parents love compliments and struggle with complaints!

Parent-teacher conferences are a great time to compliment and correct. However, too often parents tend to see only the correction side and become offended, ending any chance of growth for the student. P-T conferences are designed to help get kids on track and to get the best from them. Often, some corrections or changes do need to be made. Telling a parent that their kid isn't perfect is not an easy task. As a result, some are offended before the conference even starts!

That is why the sandwich method is powerful!

Adults can use the sandwich method to have an authentic conversation with any kid. I use it often, and kids leave my presence feeling respected and feeling good about themselves. This technique is also a great tool to use with parents.

The sandwich method is invaluable for getting an important message across. Sandwiching the corrective measure between two positive compliments often allows the critique or the area in which improvement is needed to be more considerate and benign.

## Top Slice of the Sandwich
### (The Compliment or Positive Feedback)

"Gracy is an awesome reader. We enjoy having her in our class. She takes reading seriously and excels at it. I can tell you have spent a great deal of time with her at home."

## The Filling
### (Coaching points or Criticism or Critique)

"I do feel the need to address her spelling. She seems to struggle on compound words and sounding out words. She might be the type of student who needs to spend extra time in that area. I know she can excel, but this subject might be a little harder for her than reading."

## Bottom Slice of the Sandwich
### (The Compliment or Positive Feedback)

"I know once this spelling issue is resolved, she will soar even higher. I always appreciate how hard she works and how she listens carefully during class. You should be proud of Gracy; you are doing a great job. I really appreciate your help in getting her spelling back on track."

It's amazing what you can talk about when you always start and end with a positive. Kids don't feel threatened when you start with some positive, and they are much more apt to listen to what needs to be addressed after hearing a compliment. Ending on a positive will set the stage the next time you want to talk to them.

We often try to get right to the middle—what needs some attention—without starting off with a positive affirmation. Building up the kid first and then segueing to the problem at hand won't be viewed as tearing him down. Starting and ending the conversation with praise will tear down walls so real growth can take place.

Another way I have found to model positivity is to be thankful every day.

# B. T. E.

### *B.T.E — Be Thankful Everyday!*

Kids need to see an adult who models B.T.E. We have all known B.T.E. people who exude thankfulness. Kids easily recognize people who are thankful and show gratitude.

The thankful heart of an adult will flow into kids. When times get tough, having an attitude of thankfulness will set a person apart. Kids will notice the difference, learn to develop that same attitude, and emulate the person they watched.

Throughout my life, I have been fortunate to work with some extraordinary people—mentors and co-workers who believed in me and inspired me to be the best I could be. Their teaching kids that everyone is unique and special helped build a sense of thankfulness in my life. They made gratefulness look so good, I wanted to emulate that characteristic in my life.

Having a thankful attitude will affect every aspect of a

person's life. The high speed of life often overshadows all the positive gifts for which we are to be thankful. We often forget how fortunate we are to be able to walk without pain or some type of aid or even to have dinner with our families.

A good friend of mine serves as an active-duty full-time soldier, who risks his life so we can live ours free. He is the head of his household and the father of four kids. He has been deployed three times to the Middle East. When he leaves, he says goodbye to his family for a year. I struggle with being away from my family for hours, and I cannot begin to imagine how difficult saying goodbye for a year would be.

My friend willingly serves because he believes in our country. He follows in the footsteps of all the soldiers, past and present, who have dedicated their lives for our freedom because he believes in the cause. These are real-life heroes—people our kids should be admiring and emulating.

Sick of kids looking up to pampered sports stars or millionaire singers who keep crashing and burning? Teach them who the real heroes are—these everyday people who serve others and willingly pay the price.

I believe our job is to honor and support our soldiers—the men and women who dedicate their lives to give us freedom. Kids need to know about patriotism and to be proud of the men and women who have fought and continue to fight so we can go to church and live in a democracy.

Having an attitude of gratitude starts with the adults who are mentoring this generation. Kids need to respect and be thankful every day for their freedoms, and our job is to remind them to be appreciative of the price others have paid. The next time you see a veteran or an active-duty military person, shake that hero's hand and say, "Thank you."

Kids need to see and hear adults acting grateful, and they need to learn to recognize the times they need to be thankful.

Being thankful every day makes it hard to be negative. When you step back and look at your life, I am sure you have at least one reason to smile. When kids are taught to be thankful, they pass on that attitude to everyone with whom they come in contact.

Do you really want to empower kids? Teach them to be thankful and appreciative on a daily basis. Teach them not to ignore the simple gifts in life. Teach them that heroes do exist. Teach them they have so much in their life for which to be thankful.

Working in public education has allowed me to work with some real-life heroes. I have watched these people—from superintendents to custodians—put kids first to make sure they are doing all that is possible to make them feel valued. Great people punch the time clock every day, hoping to encourage and support a child.

The struggle of daily life sometimes blinds us of all the great gifts we have. Having a B.T.E. attitude is what successful people do daily.

I know the power of seeing a B.T.E. in action, I was privileged to see this be thankful attitude firsthand.

As both a teacher and a principal, I was honored to work with the sixth grade teacher, Deborah VanHorn, who loved children. I was always impressed with her calm demeanor and understanding tone. She possessed a gift for patience, and kids admired her; she was a lighthouse.

She was very good at performing this job she loved. Her husband taught special education, and their time was spent investing in their three awesome boys. Life was her canvas, and she loved being a mom and a teacher.

We had numerous, great, meaningful conversations, but one in particular stands out above the rest. I will never forget the August day she came to my office.

The school was buzzing with teachers smiling and excited about preparing for the new school year. Everyone was in back-to-school mode. A new school year was only a couple of weeks away, and the atmosphere was static.

Mrs. VanHorn stopped in my office to update me on her summer. At first, we talked about summer traveling and our kids, but right before she left, she mentioned she had a chiropractor appointment. "I think I slept on my neck wrong, and I want to get all the kinks worked out before the school year begins."

I marveled at how Mrs. VanHorn wanted to be 100 percent ready for her next group of learners. Before she left, I commiserated with her, telling her how my neck had been stiff from sleeping wrong the night before. "I can surely relate," I ended my tale of a stiff neck. I wished her luck as she left and went back to my work.

I didn't think much about that conversation until Friday when my office phone rang, and I recognized Mrs. VanHorn's calm, soothing voice right away. "I am calling to let you know that I will be having an MRI because I am still experiencing some neck pain. The doctors want to check over a few concerns." Her call was short and to the point. I figured her next test would quickly diagnose some minor muscle soreness, and something would be prescribed to help alleviate her stiffness.

A couple of days later when my phone rang again, the message was one that I will never forget. I heard Mrs. VanHorn's same calm, soothing voice that never wavered as she told me what I couldn't believe. *Cancer?!* The MRI had revealed a fast, aggressive cancerous tumor was causing her neck pain. For one of the first times in my life, I was silent. I simply didn't know what to say.

I couldn't believe someone so young and full of life could have such a terrible disease. *How could a disease so evil be growing in a person so loving and pure?* Mrs. VanHorn had no other warning signs—just some sudden neck pain.

From that day forward, her health continued to deteriorate as the cancer spread. She went to doctor's appointment and tried all kinds of treatment options. She fought, like a champ, giving all she could to gain every minute with her boys.

Throughout that school year, I would call her every couple of weeks to talk. At first, I called her out of respect, wanting her to know that we were praying and thinking of her. I often had to compose myself because I found hearing her was not easy and not seeing her every morning in her classroom was incredibly difficult.

As we talked, her voice never wavered and never did I hear a trace of worry or anger. Our conversations continued throughout the year, and I found myself looking forward to my next phone call. I needed to hear her voice, and I needed to be encouraged by her. On bad days—on days that were filled with lampshades, I would call Mrs. VanHorn. She was always herself—loving and patient.

When her health started to deteriorate toward the end of her cancer battle, I wasn't sure how much time she had left, but she still received my calls with grace and dignity.

One of my last calls on a Tuesday morning was one that would change my life forever. Happenings at school had been hectic, and I was dealing with some issues. Negativity was mercilessly pulling at me. The lampshades were starting to get to me. I picked up the phone because I knew Mrs. VanHorn would cheer me up.

This time was different as we talked. She was quieter than normal. I knew she was not doing well. She could tell I was becoming emotional and that I was feeling sorry for her. "None of this is fair; I just feel terrible," I said. Her husband and sons were weighing heavy on mind. They loved her dearly, and her gradual decline was difficult on everyone.

At that moment when Mrs. VanHorn was in the worse position imaginable—facing her imminent death—she spoke life into me. Even in her darkest hour, she remained a lighthouse, shining her absolute brightest. Her words were so powerful, they still resonate in my soul to this day. If anyone had a reason to be negative—to be a lampshade—Mrs. Deb VanHorn did.

"I don't see it as not being fair; I am thankful," Deb replied to my outburst.

I was so shocked; I didn't know how to respond. "Thankful?" I finally managed to stammer.

"I am thankful to be married to a man I love. I am thankful to be able to be a mom to three wonderful sons. God has blessed me for all these years. Who am I to question Him now?" she asked.

"Don't be sad for me. I know where I am going; I have no doubts," she continued as confidently as anything I have ever believed in my life.

That conversation—one of the last I ever had with Mrs. VanHorn—remains permanently fixed in my most precious memories.

One of my greatest educational honors was being a pall bearer at her funeral. She had shared her light with family, colleagues and former students who had felt her positivity and came to bid her goodbye.

Wouldn't it be great if we could teach our children to live like Mrs. VanHorn—to be thankful for each day? Wouldn't it be great if we could teach them to appreciate all the blessings in their lives instead of looking for the curses? If she could live her life, even in her darkest days knowing death was knocking at the door with so much love and gratitude, why can't we?

Why can't we teach kids to love instead of hate and to build up instead of breaking down?

Deb VanHorn knew the power of positivity; she knew the importance of being thankful every day. I was fortunate enough to witness her gratefulness; I was blessed enough to know a true lighthouse.

## MAIN POINT
### *Positivity is powerful!*

## THE BIG THREE

### TIP #1

You set the tone with your attitude! Be a Lighthouse! No one wants to listen to a Lampshade.

### TIP #2

Communication is better when you start and end on a positive statement.

### TIP #3

Treat every day like a gift because it is. When you see the good in everything, kids will emulate an attitude of gratitude. Remember Mrs. Deb VanHorn; be a B-T-E.

# 10
# THE GIFT
# OF HONESTY

*Modeling
the Trait
of
Honesty*

"If you tell the truth"
you don't have
to remember anything."

– MARK TWAIN

HONESTY IS THE foundation of building healthy lasting relationships. Do you want to extinguish the fire that you have started with a student? Be dishonest! Nothing will extinguish or destroy a healthy relationship like dishonesty. Teaching children to be honest is one of the greatest gifts you can give them. Being an honest person will make them the type of parent and employee who will be successful.

Why is teaching honesty so important? For one, you will never get to the heart of a child without honesty. No problem will be solved, and no lesson will be learned unless kids realize the huge role honesty plays in their life.

Without honesty, you will not have authentic lines of communication. Children will not trust someone who isn't honest, and they will not be honest themselves if they see dishonesty modeled.

My friend, you must be the example!

Do you demonstrate honesty? If you are given too much money back at the store, do you return it or keep it? Do you tell the waiter your nine-year-old child is under the age of eight to save $2.00 on his meal?

Some may think these interactions are minor infractions of no account—that they aren't a big deal. I cannot express more strongly that they are! Every time you are dishonest or try to take advantage of a certain perk or situation, you are being watched and observed.

You cannot get upset at your child for lying when you have modeled that very behavior in restaurants or at stores. You have made lying acceptable. Kids will face a constant temptation to lie, distort the truth, and deceive others.

Kids will lie for a variety of reasons. A complete list could be a book in itself, but the following reasons are some of the more common instances when a kid may choose to lie over being honest.

- ▶ to gain something
- ▶ to try it and see what happens
- ▶ to get out of trouble
- ▶ to gain approval and self-image
- ▶ to avoid hurting someone else's feelings
- ▶ to hide something
- ▶ to protect someone else
- ▶ to gain attention
- ▶ speaking without thinking
- ▶ shifting the focus off themselves
- ▶ fear of correction
- ▶ avoidance

Knowing why kids lie is important. Sometimes an underlying, deeper, more concerning reason triggers their choice to be deceitful. Never discredit or judge a kid because he lied; he might be covering a much bigger issue about which you know nothing.

Teaching honesty to kids starts and ends with you! There are no "little white lies" when working with kids. They will see these lies thought to be insignificant and justified, remember them, and use them to their advantage. White lies are still lies! Adults who rationalize their situation by telling these untruths demonstrate their acceptability, giving kids the mindset that, in certain circumstances, lying is okay.

But not telling the truth is never acceptable.

Some of children's lying is the fault of adults. We casually make statements like "Take this medicine; it tastes good."

No! That medicine doesn't taste good! "This medicine will make you feel better" is a truthful alternative. Yes, the medicine will help you feel better, but it doesn't taste good.

## All lies need a platform

Avoid putting your child in a position to lie; don't give lying a platform. If you already know the outcome, simply give a directive. When you test kids, they will sometimes take the easy way out by choosing to lie. Eliminate the opportunity to blame or make excuses. If you know the truth, be clear and direct: *"I know you were downstairs eating cereal. Could you please go clean it up where it spilled?"*

Avoiding confrontation is an excellent way to prevent lies. When you already know the outcome, don't pretend you don't. When children are confronted, lying becomes much easier because they are scared. Telling untruths can serve as a defense mechanism that teaches kids to find the easy way out of stressful situations.

Parents should be quick to praise and slow to scold. Sometimes scolding is easier and, depending on the situation, our first response. Be proactive and praise the truth. Children love verbal praise and need to hear more. Remember, a child can never receive too much affection and pointing to the truth will reinforce self-confidence and positive behavior. Rewarding honesty with praise can be your best way to teach the value of being honest.

What do you do when a child lies? I think the more important questions is: *what don't you do?* Don't fly off the handle, thinking all they have ever told you are lies. The truth is kids lie, and sadly, so do adults. Lying, unfortunately, is a part of life, but teaching kids that lying is wrong is critically important.

When a kid lies, stay calm and be respectful. Use the offense as a teachable moment and correct the mistake. Keep in mind that the long-term goal is to develop honesty as a trait. Kids should see honesty like gold, an element long sought for its great value. A value cannot be placed on honesty.

The goal is to teach children that no matter what happens in life, they will always have their word. Giving their word is worth more than gold, and when they are dishonest, regaining that trust is difficult.

When working with kids, expect the truth. The old idiom "honesty is the best policy" should always be an adult's expectation. Telling the truth is always best—even when dishonesty would be easier.

Honesty isn't a choice. Too many times, kids will mentally debate about what to say and if they should tell the truth. Only telling the truth when it's convenient is setting them up for future lies.

Kids like expectations; in fact, they crave them. They are pleasers by nature, so make sure you are teaching honesty as an expectation—not a choice.

*Labels are for soup cans— not kids!*

Be careful not to label a child by calling them a liar or saying, "You never tell the truth." Always and never statements are seldom accurate. Labels are for soup cans—not kids!

Children will ponder the words you direct toward them, and if they hear the words enough, they will believe them. Call them a liar too many times, and they will become a liar. Telling one or two lies are bad choices but telling those one or two doesn't make them liars.

A liar can seldom be trusted.

A liar is deceitful.

"Liar" is a dangerous label to use with kids. Instead of labeling, say, "I am sorry you didn't tell the truth" or "That answer really surprises me. Usually, you are always honest with me." These words and others like them empower change and force the child to look internally without damaging their spirit. Honesty means speaking the truth.

One of the best character traits a child learns is to be honest. Learning to be honest starts at a young age and continues as they grow. Several other traits accompany honesty such as good judgment, loyalty, integrity, and courage. With honesty being the cornerstone, kids are learning some powerful attributes that will mold their character.

# EFFECTUAL WAYS TO TEACH HONESTY

1) **Define honesty.** Our words and actions must always be truthful. Honesty shows other people you are trustworthy and reliable. Talk about it, the role it plays and how important it is for people to be honest. Praising this quality should be a part of our daily vocabulary.

2) **Share your honesty journey.** Openly speak of the role honesty has played in your own life. Use your personal stories and struggles to help teach them the value of honesty and let them know that you are not perfect; you have had struggles like they do.

I always share with kids my biggest struggle with honesty occurred at a Subway when I was in college. My friend and I went in right before the restaurant closed, so only one worker was caring for the entire store. He ran out of some condiments and had to go to the storeroom. As he left, I noticed a giant roll of free Subway stamps laying on the counter. For a split second, I thought about grabbing the Subway stamps and leaving. I would have been eating free submarine sandwiches for the next five years! Thankfully my conscience won, and I left the stamps, but I was sorely tempted.

Sharing these circumstances show kids you have battled some of the same temptations they have in everyday life.

**3) Brainstorm consequences.** What happens when a person is dishonest? Present real-life examples or use a story from a book to illustrate the consequences that each character is faced with after choosing to lie. Look through media sources and share appropriate instances where recognizable people were faced with a moral dilemma and chose to lie.

Explain that people who are a part of their life will lose trust in them. Usually, one lie turns into two and so on. For students to see characters or people who face consequences as a result of being dishonest can be a powerful deterrent.

**4) Use a moral vocabulary.** Teaching kids that honesty can come in multiple words and actions is important to building character. Be sure to connect these additional words you are using in your daily vocabulary to honesty. For example, words like *honor, integrity, morals, nobility,* and *ethics* are all related to honesty. The more you include these words in your vocabulary, the more they will become etched into a kid's mind. Plan activities for kids and instruct them to find other ways to represent the quality of honesty.

**5) People aren't mind readers.** Honesty prevents other people from trying to read your mind and figure out what you are thinking and feeling. When it comes to feelings, being honest will help solve problems instead of promoting them. Honesty can bring healing to someone who has been hurt, renew relationships, and provide hope. Honesty can also open the door for good communication.

Kids who realize the many positive benefits to living an honest life and embrace honesty will help their peers and adults from having to guess how they feel. Embracing the quality of honesty will be a strong attribute to a healthy, happy life. The person who doesn't know the truth will try to guess, and this guessing can lead to negativity and gossip, which can lead to more lies. All of this dishonesty could have been avoided with honesty.

6) Be "the airport." Adults should always encourage kids to be honest. Always provide a safe place or a runway for a kid to tell the truth. If kids are confronted with dishonesty in front of a class or among friends, they will often make a poor choice because they feel they don't have an honest way out of the problem. Give them a way so they don't feel judged, trapped, or embarrassed. Clinical psychologist Mary Alice Silverman says, "There is at least a 50% chance they will be dishonest to avoid getting into trouble."[1] Adults need to try to eliminate that 50 percent chance and help them take the high road.

7) Start with the truth. I like to start difficult questions with the truth. As a principal at school, I always start with the truth when having a challenging conversation with kids. I say, "I promise to be honest and fair with you. Can you make me the same promise and be honest and fair with me?" I use this tactic because they hear that I will be just, and I provide my expectations within the framework of our conversation. I also

add, "I value your time, and the more honest we are, the more quickly we can resolve this matter."

Honesty is one of the most important moral traits our kids will need in life. At some point in your life, you have no doubt been hurt by dishonesty. As I have already stated, being dishonest undermines trust and is detrimental in forming lasting healthy relationships with others. Honesty provides the voice that builds trust and context. These examples will create an honest atmosphere at school, home, or in whatever endeavor you have the privilege of mentoring kids. By the life you live, kids will recognize and incorporate the value of honesty and learn how to avoid being dishonest.

# MAIN POINT

*Being honest allows a kid to be prepared when trouble comes and be successful in resisting the temptation to tell a lie.*

# THE BIG THREE

TIP #1:

The best way to teach kids to be honest is to be honest yourself!

TIP #2:

Avoid lies—even "little white lies." A white lie is a lie.

TIP #3:

Labels are for soup cans; never call a child a liar.

# 11
# HIGH EXPECTATIONS;
# HIGH RESULTS

*Knowing the
Importance
of Setting
High Goals*

"High expectations
are the key to everything."

– SAM WALTON,
*Walmart Founder*

W HEN YOU BELIEVE in kids, they will believe in themselves. You should set high standards for kids. Investing and impacting kids requires that you have the mindset that they are capable of reaching their greatest potential. Each individual kid will have his own different "best," but we must believe in and help them to be the very best they can be. Kids will either live up to or down to your expectations.

Creating and maintaining high expectations can sometimes be a controversial topic in today's world. As I stated in a previous chapter, we now live in a world that wants everyone to win the blue ribbon. Parity never works in a classroom setting; initiative and creativity are destroyed.

Do some people create unrealistic expectations or put too much pressure on kids? Of course, but those mistakes don't downplay the key role that high expectations play in the success in a kid's life.

Set realistic goals that a kid will do all he can do to obtain. Our world is trending away from high expectations because people get uncomfortable with consequences.

Didn't study for a test? There is a natural consequence—a low grade.

Didn't put in extra work on the basketball court? Don't complain when the tryouts don't go your way.

The world is filled with consequences, so having high expectations for kids establishes firm goals and boundaries for them. Human nature will have kids testing the rules until they find clear boundaries and consequences.

Parenting is the most difficult job you will ever find. There is nothing on this earth I love the same as my children. As a parent, I want to protect them, I want the best for them, and I want them to be joyful. I also want them to be accountable. I want them to set high goals and work hard to achieve them. I want them to know that no matter what happens in this world, I will always love them and care for them.

My job is to teach my children what authentic caring is.

Caring doesn't mean that I continue to give chance after chance or look the other way to excuse poor choices or bad habits. Making excuses for or justifying a mistake does not do any child a favor.

Having high expectations lays the foundation for a kid to have a mindset of growth. Establishing high expectations helps a child create an atmosphere where achievement is based on doing their best.

Does one child's best look different than someone else's? Absolutely!

Expectations allow each kid to strive to achieve his best. Having and raising expectations that have been met stretches a child to reach for greater goals. The goal of establishing high expectation ultimately leads to a better self-belief and a foundation built on hard work.

I have seen countless positive examples of expectations

met in the classroom and on various sports fields. Teachers who promote and value high expectations have a greater impact on kids and typically see better academic results.

Why? Kids will learn faster and improve when they know someone believes they can. Having high expectations tell kids that you "can" and "will" do it! Your belief in kids and setting the bar high tells them, "You can achieve this goal, and here is how you will achieve it!"

The following are some examples of the different approaches when expectations are low and what happens when expectations are high.

## Common Traits with Low Expectations

- ▶ Constantly reminding kids of expectations and routine
- ▶ Manages behavior by reacting in mostly negative ways
- ▶ Believes achievement is ability
- ▶ Uses direct questioning with limited answers

## Common Traits with High Expectations

- ▶ Clear goals and expectations are in place; few reminders are needed
- ▶ Manages behavior proactively, stays positive
- ▶ Believes achievement is based on motivation, effort, and goals
- ▶ Asks open-ended questions that encourage kids' own ideas

---

# ADAPTING AND MODELING A MIND-SET OF HIGH EXPECTATIONS

These examples can be modified or applied at home, school, church, the athletic arena, or anyplace where kids traditionally spend time.

**1) A direct way to communicate high expectations is by establishing clear rules, routines, and procedures.** Incorporating and giving kids a voice in the process works best. When I taught fifth grade, instead of handing out a list of rules for the classroom, I asked my students to help me create them. We talked about what was important to them and made them feel comfortable. Every year, the same basic rules were established, but consulting with my students gave them ownership and voice. Basically, on the first day, they set their own expectations.

If you, as a teacher, are unplanned and unprepared, the kids will eat you alive. Establish and adhere to the rules and expectations that are created.

Thinking about instituting a chore chart at home? Sit down as a family and ask what chores they value and why they are valued. The discussion will eventually allow kids to see why even the most despised of mundane chores need to be done.

**2) To have high expectations, you must first believe that each child is capable and able to achieve the goal.** Poet James Allen said, "The oak sleeps in the acorn." You must first believe that every child is an acorn waiting to sprout into a glorious, majestic oak tree. This sprouting and growing might take time

---

as some soil might need more preparation, but each one will become an oak tree.

This expression doesn't apply only to high-achieving super kids. This phrase applies to every single kid. Every kid possesses the potential to grow into something special.

I believe that mindset in every kid starts with one person believing in him and instilling within him a mindset of having high expectations. Our job is to believe that each kid can, then establish high expectations outlining how they will achieve their dreams. Kids are influenced by the expectations placed before them.

One of the most well-known case studies that links high teacher expectations to improved students' results is known as the Pygmalion Effect.[1] In 1968 researchers Robert Rosenthal and Lenore Jacobson conducted a study focused on the correlation between a teacher's expectations and the results among the students. The study took place in an elementary school in California. Students took a disguised intelligence pre-test in the fall.

The teachers were given the names of 20 percent of the students who showed unusual potential for intellectual growth. As the ones with the most potential, they would be the so-called high risers in the classroom.

However, unknown to the teachers, the names of the students were randomly drawn and had no connection to the original test. When the same students were tested again eight months later, their test scores were significantly higher.

Rosenthal explained that when certain behaviors are expected of others, they are likely to act in ways that make those expected behaviors more likely to occur. The Rosenthal-Jacobson findings reveal how high expectations can lead to good results. People do better when more is expected of them.

Failure is not an option, so never predict it. A simple way to communicate high expectations is by making failing unacceptable. Never forecast failure with a child. When we accept a child's failure, we give them the option to accept it as well. When adults believe in and encourage children, they will start to believe in themselves.

# TEN STRATEGIES FOR HIGH EXPECTATIONS

1. Be firm and consistent.

2. Teach that effort is the excellence.

3. Create a growth mindset.

4. Model high expectations for yourself.

5. Ask open-ended questions and listen to the responses.

6. Contribute achievable but attainable difficult tasks.

7. Give examples when correcting.

8. Make sure your praise is worth praising.

9. Never allow a kid to give up.

10. Don't use gimmicks or try to trick kids.

In her book, *Mindset: How You Can Fulfill Your Potential*, Carol Dweck explains researcher Falko Rheinberg's work about the differences between a fixed mindset versus a growth mindset. Her book offers specific strategies and data regarding the power of a growth mindset.

Rheinberg's study focused on a student's academic achievement and progress, as well as the role expectations played in achievement. He discovered that teachers who believe that students have a fixed mindset ended the year at the same level they started. Little to no academic growth took place for the entire year. A student in the bottom tier of a class ended in the same place, showing no progress or advancement after a calendar year of school.

The students taught by teachers with a growth mindset (or a belief that it didn't matter where a student started; he could still achieve higher levels) grew tremendously, advancing positively. A much higher movement occurred in ability groups as students learned and felt approval. Studies show that students are directly influenced by the mindset of the teacher.

Rheinberg's findings revealed a direct correlation with the teacher's expectations and the academic achievement of their students. Teachers who had a fixed mindset saw little to no growth in their students, whereas the students of teachers with a growth mindset and high expectations progressed to greater heights than where they began.

Rheinberg's study revealed a direct correlation between high expectations and high results. Research showed that growth-minded people equipped with better problem-solving techniques are happier, more successful, more productive, and more focused. Having high expectations is a huge component of a growth mindset. What matters is not where a kid starts, but where he will be.

**3) Start by developing an attitude that all kids are capable of high expectations.** Know that one kids' best is different than another's, but differences do not take away from the fact they can reach high goals. When kids know that you have high standards, they will soon start setting the bar higher for themselves.

# MAIN POINT

*Having realistic high expectations for kids
tells them you believe in them.*

# THE BIG THREE

TIP #1

The goal of having high expectations is creating a mindset based on self-belief and hard work.

TIP #2

Never predict or make excuses for failure. Instead, prepare them to do their best by believing in themselves and through establishing high expectations for them.

TIP #3

Believe that each child is an acorn waiting to sprout into a fabulous oak tree. Remind them, push them, and believe in them.

# 12
# THE POWER OF THE "E"

*Evoking
Empathy
over
Entitlement*

"The purpose of human life is to serve,
and to show compassion
and the will to help others."

– ALBERT SCHWEITZER

"I WANT IT!" Those thoughts are etched onto every child's mind the minute they can talk. Don't believe me? Take a five-year old through the toy aisle at your local Walmart. Drive around a used car parking lot with your soon to be 16 year old. Humans are wired to want items—especially nice items. While wanting luxuries is a part of life; the feeling that they are owed to them is not.

Society doesn't help with this concept. Every time the television is turned on, commercials air with the newest, greatest toy every kid absolutely must have. When kids are school age, other peers will influence what they wear and how they wear it. You know the line: you're not cool unless you wear Brand X clothes. This constant barrage of commercialism and materialism is part of the reason why so many kids are falling prey to a sense of entitlement.

Don't get me wrong! All kids and adults will have luxuries they want. Nothing is wrong with rewarding an achievement or with working hard and saving toward its purchase. But giving an item or earning an item is profoundly different.

## ENTITLEMENT

Entitlement is the attitude that a kid should get an item when he wants because he wants it—not because he deserves it. For example, he has not worked hard to have the privilege of living in your house nor has he helped you with paying all the bills. Quite the contrary! This idea of social peer pressure and television often make parents try to overcompensate for their kids. They think, "If I just give them more, they will be happy. They will think I am cool."

I personally do not want my kids to be like everyone else; I want them to be them! I want them to understand that effort and hard work is the way to earn luxuries. Nothing in life will simply be given to them because of who they are. That false sense of entitlement not only hurts your family, it is hurting generations of families. Someday your son or daughter will be parents, so now is the time to start teaching them dangers of a false sense of entitlement.

"Earn it; don't expect it" needs to be the message to your children. "You want it? Do the work to get it."

When I was younger, my parents made me mow the grass with a walk-behind mower—not the self-propelled kind where all I had to do was guide it. I had to provide the power to push the mower. I hated the job and frequently complained about the work that caused everything from hurting feet to a heart attack! My parents even offered to pay me $10 for completing the job, but every time I complained or made an excuse, they deducted some money from my pay.

I cannot count how many times I ended up cutting the grass for free. Sometimes I even owed them more money than when I had started mowing! My attitude change didn't happen overnight, but eventually I realized that they didn't owe me a dime, and I was the one responsible for forfeiting my pay! I still had to cut the grass and after many hard lessons, I realized making $10 was better than cutting it for free. No matter what, I still had to cut the grass. What my parents were trying to teach me was simple:

- ▶ Learn the value of earning money because money doesn't come easy.

- ▶ Hard work is a part of life. If you really want something, earn it.

- ▶ Because you're our son and we love you doesn't mean you don't have to work.

- ▶ They set limits with consequences.

Allowing kids to have a false sense of entitlement does not prepare them for the real world. When money and material items have always been given to them, they won't know what it means to work hard or to struggle. Teaching them the value of hard word doesn't start when they enter high school. It starts now—today!

So how do you battle entitlement? How do you raise kids to value hard work and money? You teach them to value the greatest asset on earth—people.

While teaching that entitlement can be a dangerous "E," also teach them about the most important "E's".

# EMPOWERMENT

The word *empowerment* brings a variety of thoughts and feelings to people. After all, our society has almost made empowerment or empowering a political cause.

My purpose is not to address that type of empowering; rather, the type of empowering I want to promote is how you impact and encourage other people or yourself. When I say we need to empower kids, I simply mean we need to help kids believe they can accomplish tasks and handle setbacks and obstacles while continuing to achieve.

Basically, empowerment in kids means we believe in them. We believe they have the ability and potential to be anything they set their mind to be.

This type of empowerment teaches your child to appreciate people and their hard work ethic. Imparting this outlook has to start with *you*. Every second you spend with your kids is a teachable moment because they are watching and listening to all that you say and do. One of the greatest skills you can teach your child is empowerment, so make sure you are modeling this trait.

The greatest leaders already model this trait. How many NBA championships did Michael Jordan win without Scottie Pippen? The answer is simple—zero. Jordan had to help develop and build Pippen into an All-Star. The results were amazing. Six NBA Championship titles later, the importance of empowering others around you was obvious. Certainly, empowering others doesn't have to be done on such a grand scale.

It's simple! Open the door for people and let them enter first. Be polite to the waitstaff even when the food brought after a long late doesn't taste good. Don't be someone who says, "Do as I say—not as I do." I have talked to so many adults who question why their kid got in trouble for cursing as they constantly swear during our conversation. Truly, behaviors such as swearing are learned and modeled.

Kids will do exactly what they see their parents do, and they will repeat what their parents say. Parents model behavior for their children, and their children will learn how to live life by their parents' actions.

Empower kids by complimenting often and complaining less. After all, the best way to compensate for complaining is to compliment others. Always be genuine, kind, and truthful in your compliments.

# EMPATHY

Another way to combat a false sense of entitlement is by teaching kids the value of empathy. Teach them to care for other people and to be aware of other people's feelings.

Entitlement says, "It's all about me."

Empathy says, "It's about others."

*Empathy* is the ability to understand other people's feelings and act in a helpful way. While some children seem to naturally develop a sense of empathy, this skill still needs to be modeled and taught. Not only will developing children's empathy help them understand their own feelings, but proper coping mechanisms will also be created to apply when they are having difficult times. Children who are empathetic are less like to bully and more likely to have coping skills.

Empathy will help teach responsibility; children will depend less on impulse and more on thought. These problem-solving skills will carry on and help build a loving, caring person. Learning to recognize empathy will also help develop problem-solving skills in a child. Once children learn empathy, they will feel the need to help others who are suffering. Every day opportunities to teach empathy and empowerment are presented. Don't let these moments slip away, and make sure your kids know the power and dangers of the "E," and instead embrace the wonderful attributes of empathy.

A kid who is empathic and empowered will live courageously. He will radiate confidence. So many kids suffer from anxiety mostly due to the uncertainty of their future. Anxious kids want reassurance and answers from others when they are presented with fear.

In 2006 a young senator from Illinois and the future President of the United States, Barack Obama, felt called to highlight the importance of teaching empathy. He felt in order to make the world a better place, the importance of empathy needed to be stressed.

I think we should talk more about the empathy deficit— the ability to put ourselves in someone else's shoes, to see the world through the eyes of those who are different from us—the child who's hungry, the steelworker who's been laid off, the family who lost the entire life they built together when the storm came to town. When you think like this, when you choose to broaden your ambit of concern and empathize with the plight of the others— whether they are close friends or distant strangers—it becomes harder not to act, harder not to help.[1]

Teaching kids to have empathy helps them understand and see a variety of perspectives. Kids are also equipped to have appropriate responses when problems arise. Maya Angelou said, "I think we all have empathy. We may not have enough courage to display it."[2] Encouraging kids to recognize and embrace empathy will not only make them more empathetic, it will also make them problem solvers instead of problem starters.

## DAILY WAYS TO MODEL AND TEACH EMPATHY

▶ **Talk about feelings and emotions.** Having kids recognize their feelings are natural and not taboo to discuss will promote empathy. For kids to know that talking about feelings is acceptable will allow them to be comfortable with their feelings and help them regulate their emotions.

▶ **Language is a choice.** Make sure your language reflects an empathetic tone; avoid labeling or using negative tones to describe another's emotions. Sounding too judgmental or using language that devalues a kid's feelings will diminish his perspective of empathy. Being aware of your language also teaches kids the power of both positive and negative talk.

▶ **Use *compare* and *contrast* statements.** The ability to identify people's behavior and feelings is a great teaching tool. Relating to or sensing familiarity in other people help teach empathy. Point out similarities that kids share to help build a greater range of empathy. Being able to recognize similarities will also enable a kid to be supportive of others when adversity or tragedy strikes. By using compare and contrast statements, you are laying down future groundwork and developing skills when challenges come.

► **Serve others.** Stress the value of service and compassion. Teaching kids the value of compassion will be a major factor in building empathy. Expose kids to local opportunities to serve their community and the people who live there. Numerous school organizations volunteer and provide community service. Take kids to retirement homes to sing, do crafts, or to have simple conversations with the residents. Food drives are an excellent way to serve others and see a different perspective of how some people live. Expanding kids' view of people and the positive effect they can have will expand their perspective.

► **Identify feelings with emotions.** Acknowledging a kid's feelings and their connection to his emotions is so important. Depending on the ages of kids, their emotions manifest in different ways. Crying may be an emotion younger children show when scared, angry, or sad. In older kids, crying could be the result of having a high level of anxiety or frustration. Even though the emotion is the same, the feeling may be completely different. Connecting the feeling with the emotion will allow you to have an authentic conversation about what is really bothering the kid. This idea of cause and effect will help make kids analyze the situation and make empathetic connections for both themselves and others.

► **Authentically apologize.** An apology is powerful for those involved. The hope is that the person or persons offended will accept the apology and move on feeling better. Too often we force kids to apologize simply to apologize. A half-hearted mumbled apology because they were told to do so is not an apology. Kids can see through that mumbled effort, and the offense isn't repaired because they knew the apology was insincere.

Teach kids to own their apology and understand why they are apologizing. It is easy to see and feel an authentic apology. Giving an authentic apology is a skill kids often struggle with doing. Limit excuses and stick strictly to the facts.

▶ **Avoid the trap of social media.** Social media can have a damaging effect on a kid's view of empathy. Kids are seeing and being exposed to negativity through inappropriate social media. Depending on age and maturity, talking to kids about social media is essential. Social media has added a whole new level of challenges for kids as they are exposed and bombarded with inappropriateness. Don't think simply because a kid is young, he is immune. They are not!

Pop-up ads and in game videos have made monitoring what is being seen and heard on social media a nightmare for parents and teachers. Kids need to know that what is posted on social media is permanent. Their posts may disappear, but they are "there" forever.

Try to have them put themselves in the other person's shoes on the other side of the screen and ask themselves, "Why are they writing or posting what they are?" Ask them searching questions: "How do you think your parents or loved ones would feel about a posted picture or a comment if they saw it?"

"How would they feel about comments posted in the past ten years?"

▶ **Go "old school."** A powerful way to reflect and show empathy for others is for kids to hand write or type a personal thank-you note. These notes provoke kids to think about the person they are writing and a great way to show gratitude. Recognizing why you are thankful for others is a great way to personally reflect on why you are thankful for them.

Have kids think of someone who made a positive impact in their life and have them write a letter to that person. Reflect on all the characteristics and reasons why this person came to mind. Recognizing the traits they see as valuable in other people could cause them to treasure those same traits.

———

Kids need to know that entitlement is dangerous and counterproductive to their goals. When kids feel empowered and have empathy, they are able to make informed decisions based on themselves and the possible consequences. They will be able to make safer decisions, relate better to people, and handle their emotions. Empowerment and empathy—two of the most powerful tools kids can have in their emotional toolbox—can help them have less anxiety, make friends easier, prevent bullying, and help others.

---

# MAIN POINT

*Kids need to feel empowered and build empathy to improve their mental health and help develop healthy relationships.*

# THE BIG THREE

### TIP #1

Entitlement is dangerous and diminishes kids' work ethic.

### TIP #2

When kids become empowered, it allows them to impact and encourage those around them.

### TIP #3

Empathy teaches kids to see someone else's perspective. Having empathy creates better problem-solving skills for kids.

---

# CONCLUSION

KIDS NEED AS many positive influences as possible in their life. Being able to be a difference maker in a kid's life is one of the most rewarding experiences any adult will ever have.

While I will never be on the cover of the *Wall Street Journal* or be a young millionaire, I know that the intrinsic rewards are worth so much more than all the money in the world. I have had the privilege of being responsible for the happiness and outcomes of so many young people. Kids will always remember the adults in their lives who helped light their fire. Oftentimes we work with the seeds and don't get to see the kids bloom into successful adults, but we are witnesses to so many euphoric lifetime events. We are witnesses to so many firsts.

Kids will remember. They will hold dear the time you dressed up as their favorite character of their book. They will never forget when you were there for them during a difficult time. You receive your pay in smiles and aha moments that fill your intrinsic bank account.

You might not know it yet, but you are a daily lifesaver for a kid.

Will working with kids be frustrating and stressful at times? Of course! But investing in kids will always be worth the effort. I have never questioned my role and the immense responsibility I have had as an educator.

I get to be inspiring and impactful every day! I can think of no bigger job in this world than being able to impact kids. The children of today are the future adults of tomorrow who will continue to shape our world.

A couple of years ago, I received an email from a former student of mine. *Remember Sam?* I recognized his name as soon as I saw it pop into my inbox. A number of great and not-so-great memories ran through my mind as I thought about my year with this challenging student.

In fact, Sam was one of the most challenging students I have ever had in my teaching career. When he was in my fifth-grade class, he was having to cope with some deep-seated issues that needed professional help. I remember begging my principal to find Sam some help. Unfortunately, she encountered roadblock after roadblock as she sought to find that needed professional help for Sam.

Years later I heard that Sam's life had spiraled down a dark road. He had attempted to take his own life only to survive a gunshot wound to the face. As a result, Sam's already difficult life became much harder as he rehabbed and worked to regain basic daily tasks. His failed attempt put him in an even harder place in this world.

I was very surprised to hear from Sam after 15 years or so had passed. His email was short and to the point. He reached out to me to thank me for believing in him and for never giving up on him. Tears started to well in my eyes as I thought about him as student in my class when blurting out, arguing, and having meltdowns had been common occurrences.

However, those weren't the memories that immediately flooded my mind. I remembered his hugging me and saying, "I love you, Mr. Walker." I remembered his sideways crooked smile when he answered a math question correctly. Sam had entered my class in my second year of teaching when I was incredibly naïve and had yet to learn so much more about education. I wished that I would have been able to be his teacher when I was older, wiser, and had more training.

Another thought then hit me: Sam's email wasn't about my being a *better* teacher. Whatever we did in the classroom during his fifth-grade year worked to light the fire and caused him to reconnect with me again so many years later. I realized that I was already using many of the strategies and ideas that are presented in the pages of this book.

I believed in Sam. Even though he was often a rascal, I had high expectations for him. I noticed him. I refused to be offended when he had one of his many outbursts. I believed that Sam's environment did not have to dictate his future.

Out of all the teachers and people in his life, Sam remembered me and thought enough of me to send an email thanking me. His email fanned the flames of my fire and reinforced what I knew in my soul: kids need us.

They need someone to smile at them and tell them they are worth it. Sam's email made me realize the power that one caring adult can have in a kid's life. That email proved to me that "If you build it, they will come."

After wiping away the tears, I replied and thanked him for his email.

My experiences with Sam taught me never to go to bed angry and how foolish holding a grudge against a kid was. Sam was the one with whom I had prepared to do battle. The next day of school, he had merely greeted me with a hello and a smile like nothing had even happened the day before.

Sam had taught me, and he had allowed me to learn. I had other kids like him, but I was prepared. I was determined that no matter the variables, I was going to utilize all of my power to light the fire of every kid with whom I came in contact. He was one whose fire was the most difficult to start; it was full of wet wood and barely sparked.

Today, Sam's fire burns bright.

# END NOTES

CHAPTER 2 — *If You Build It, They Will Come*
[1]Rita Pierson as quoted in "Culturally Responsive Teaching for Significant Relationships by Sarah Edwards and Nancy A. Edick, *CiteSeer,* 2013, http://citeseerx.ist.psu.edu/viewdoc/summary?doi=10.1.1.825.3493.

[2]Carlton Ashby, "Three Keys to Student Success: Relationships, Relationships, Relationships," *Education World,* 2008, https://www.educationworld.com/a_admin/columnists/ashby/ashby001.shtml.

[3]Phil Alden Robinson, director, *Field of Dreams,* Universal Studios, 1989, DVD.

CHAPTER 3 — *Footprints of Heroes*
[1]Fred Rogers, Fred Rogers Center, *Facebook,* October 11, 2017, https://www.facebook.com/FredRogersCenter/posts/we-live-in-a-world-in-which-we-need-to-share-responsibility-its-easy-to-say-its-/10155841685828069/.

[2]Rita Pierson, "Every Kid Needs a Champion," *TED Talks,* May 3, 2013, YouTube, https://www.youtube.com/watch?v=SFnMTHhKdkw.

Chapter 4 — *Bring the H.E.A.T.*

[1]Deep Patel, "What These 5 Billionaires Would Tell Their Younger Selves," *Entrepreneur,* November 19, 2018, https://www.entrepreneur.com/article/323130.

Chapter 5 — *The Eagle and the Snake*

[1]"Nine Affects, Present at Birth, Combine with Life Experience to Form Emotion and Personality," *The Tomkins Institute,* 2014, http://www.tomkins.org/what-tomkins-said/introduction/nine-affects-present-at-birth-combine-to-form-emotion-mood-and-personality.

[2]*Ibid.*

[3]"Defining Restorative: Nine Affects," *IIRP Graduate School,* 2021, https://www.iirp.edu/defining-restorative/nine-affects.

[4]Therese Borchard, "Words Can Change Your Brain," *Everyday Health*, August 13, 2013, https://www.everydayhealth.com/columns/therese-borchard-sanity-break/420/.

[5]"Andrew B. Newberg Quotes," *Goodreads*, 2021, https://www.goodreads.com/author/quotes/3893926.Andrew_B_Newberg.

Chapter 6 — *"Can You Hear Me Now?"*

[1]"Epictetus Quotes," *Goodreads,* 2021, https://www.goodreads.com/quotes/738640-we-have-two-ears-and-one-mouth-so-that-we.

[2]Stephen Covey, "Using Empathic Listening to Collaporate," *Culture of Empathy*, http://cultureofempathy.com/References/Experts/Stephen-Covey.htm.

[3]"Bryant H. McGill Quotes," *BrainyQuote*, 2021, https://www.brainyquote.com/quotes/bryant_h_mcgill_168254.

[4]"Michael Caine Quotes," *BrainyQuote*, 2021, https://www.brainyquote.com/quotes/michael_caine_140815.

CHAPTER 7 — *Mirror, Mirror on the Wall*

[1]Brené Brown as quoted by Rinku Shanker, "Raising a Confident Child," August 14, 2020, *Serene Psychological Services, LLC,* https://www.serenepsych.com/post/what-causes-sleep-anxiety.

CHAPTER 8 — *Not Everyone Gets a Blue Ribbon*

[1]"48 Famous Failures Who Will Inspire You to Achieve," *Wanderlust Worker,* https://www.wanderlustworker.com/48-famous-failures-who-will-inspire-you-to-achieve.

CHAPTER 10 — *The Gift of Honesty*

[1]Mary Alice Silverman as quoted in "8 Ways Parents Can Teach Teens to Be Honest," May 11, 2017, *PressReader,* https://www.pressreader.com/south-africa/daily-news-south-africa/20170511/282892320574580.

CHAPTER 11 — *High Expectations = High Results*

[1]Ulrich Boser et al, "The Power of the Pygmalion Effect," Cener for American Progress," October 6, 2014, https://www.americanprogress.org/issues/education-k-12/reports/2014/10/06/96806/the-power-of-the-pygmalion-effect/.

CHAPTER 12 — *The Power of "E"*

[1]Barack Obama, "Xavier University Commencement Address,"

transcript of speech delivered at Xavier University, New Orleans, LA, August 11, 2016, obamaspeeches.com/087-Xavier-University-Commencement-Address-Obama-Speech.htm.

[2]"Maya Angelou Quotes," *Brainy Quote*, 2021, https://www.brainyquote.com/quotes/maya_angelou_578832.

# ABOUT THE AUTHOR

L ANE WALKER IS an award-winning author, educator, and speaker. Walker started his career as a fifth-grade teacher and then segued into education leadership serving as an elementary school principal. The past seven years, he has been a C.T.E. Director/Principal at a Career Technical Center. Lane paid his way through college working as a news and sports reporter for a newspaper. After college, he combined his love for writing and the outdoors. For the past 20 years, he has been an outdoor writer and has published over 250 articles in various newspapers and magazines. His first book collection, *Hometown Hunters* (six books) was awarded a Moonbeam Bronze Medal for Children's Best Book Series.

In 2021, his second book collection, *The Fishing Chronicles* (five books), was released and awarded a Gold Medal Moonbeam for first place Children's Best Book Series. Lane's book sales have put him in the top 1 percent of all authors.

He has a passion for inspiring and impacting kids. He celebrates the fact that he is serving in education and can make a daily impact in a kid's life.

Lane is a proud husband and dad to four children. He has

served on many princpal committes and advisory boards. He is also a highly sought-after public speaker.

To learn more about Lane Walker, visit his website:

www.lanewalker.com